RUNAWAY!

. . . Gene went to the door just in time to see our daughter run into the cul-de-sac and disappear.

"Jill, Jill, come back!" Gene called.

We stood there stunned, feeling frightened and angry. Too confused to think what to do next. Then Eddie's car started, and we watched it pull back onto the boulevard across from our house.

"She's in his car! I know she's in that car!" I screamed. "Make him stop and get her out of there!"

Gene ran across the median toward the car. Eddie stopped and got out. Now I was afraid of what he might do. Pictures of things I had read about kids on drugs raced through my mind. Gene could see that Jill was not in the car.

"Make him open the trunk. She probably crawled into the trunk." My voice seemed eerie and unreal. . . .

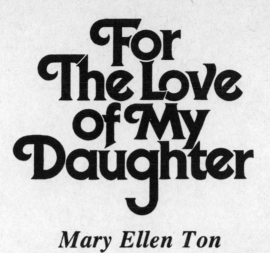

For The Love of My Daughter

Mary Ellen Ton

David C. Cook Publishing Co.

ELGIN, ILLINOIS—WESTON, ONTARIO
FULLERTON, CALIFORNIA

ACKNOWLEDGMENTS
Credit and appreciation are due publishers and copyright owners for
the use of:
"On Children" reprinted from THE PROPHET, by Kahlil Gibran,
with permission of the publisher, Alfred A. Knopf, Inc. Copyright
1923 by Kahlil Gibran; renewal copyright 1951 by Administrators
C. T. A. of Kahlil Gibran Estate, and Mary G. Gibran.

FOR THE LOVE OF MY DAUGHTER

Published by David C. Cook Publishing Co., Elgin, IL 60120
Edited by Janet Hoover Thoma
Printed in the United States of America

Library of Congress Catalog Number: 77-87253
ISBN: 0-89191-104-9

First printing—February 1978
Second printing—May 1978
Third printing—October 1978
Fourth printing—January 1979
Fifth printing—May 1979

To Gene,
who builds bridges instead of walls.

CONTENTS

PREFACE

"I'VE HAD IT!" my friend exploded. "I can't take any-more. I'm through with God . . . the church . . . every-thing."

How familiar her words sounded. But what could I say? I'd been there. I knew how it felt to have a daughter run away. Sure, this time she knew Linda was going. But what's the difference? The hurt, the disappointment, the sense of utter failure were the same.

All the old feelings came back. The cold, hard fear clutched at my stomach; the heaviness grew in my chest, making it hard to breathe; the dreaded, something-awful-is-going-to-happen anxiety returned. I leaned back in the small bedroom chair and reminded myself that it was all over. My daughter wasn't running away.

But as my friend continued to talk about her crisis, I couldn't help continuing to think about my own Jill. I assured myself that she was at work and would soon be returning to her apartment. The feelings subsided, and I wanted to tell our story to my friend. I tried. But she wasn't ready to hear it yet. I wondered if she would find a light at the end of her tunnel as I had.

A day or so earlier I had been asked to write a resume for this book. It would be the story of a badly fractured relationship—of rebellion, frustration, and anger, of the weapons we used to hurt one another, and the wall we built between us. But it would also be a story of hope. And that is what I wanted to give my friend that day. Her phone call was the encouragement I needed to move ahead.

Perhaps there is no greater heartbreak for parents than when their child rejects all the values that are a part of their life. Within the last year, four families in our church have gone through this kind of experience, four families that I know of. How many others, I can only guess. One father had a police band radio. He heard the call to pick up our daughter. But he never spoke of it until two years later when he found himself in a similar situation. Tears streamed down his face as he shared his anguish with my husband. He said he came because he knew we would understand. We did, and we do.

And that is why I have had the audacity to begin. I know nothing about writing a book. But I do know the pain many parents are experiencing. I know about watching a child turn into a complete stranger, about waiting up for someone who doesn't return, about the fear of drugs and sex, and the wanting to do something—anything—but not knowing what to do or where to turn. I know, too, what is occurring in some counseling situations. Parents struggling with unbearable guilt turn to counseling for support, encouragement, and some kind of help. Instead, the blame is laid squarely on them.

I want to share our story with these parents. And I

want to share the freedom I came to know. For the worst is not the hurt, the fear, the humiliation—not even the separation. It is the guilt, the feeling that they are responsible for the choices their child is making. I felt life being crushed out of me, until God reached me in some strange and marvelous ways.

This is not a "they-lived-happily-ever-after" story. There were no magic solutions . . . no instant cures. But there were some insights that might be a source of encouragement to other parents. And there was a lot of growing. Out of it all came hope.

RUNAWAY

1

"WE'VE PICKED UP YOUR DAUGHTER. Will you come get her?" The voice on the other end of the line spoke matter-of-factly. To him, it was an everyday happening. I was suddenly cold and trembling, even though it was August.

"Where did you find her?" I was finally able to ask. His response confirmed my worst thoughts.

"She was picked up at the Greer Motel on Route 41."

I could not remember my husband's phone number at the church, and I had difficulty locating it in the phone book. I dialed—the wrong number. "Oh, God," I said, and with the words came tears and some release of the moment's tension. I dialed again, and Gene answered. There was a solidness in it. Something to grab hold of...

By the time he reached our house, I was numb. We said very little during the twenty-minute ride downtown. But when we got out of the car and walked toward the City-County Building, my heart beat out a frightened rhythm. The pounding was so hard I was conscious of every thump. I had lived forty years without ever entering a police station. Now my daughter was being held some-where in this huge building.

We stopped at the information desk to ask directions. My mouth was dry, and my palms wet. I realized it was not anxiety I felt but plain fear. I was afraid of this place, of the policeman who pointed us down the hall to the juvenile division, of what would happen next.

Our runaway child sat on a bench along one wall. Dirty, bare feet. Her jeans torn. The long hair she was so proud of hung limp and stringy about her face. Her cheeks were mascara-streaked and red and blotchy. She had been crying. But not now. Now her face was hard—so hard.

My beautiful little ponytailed girl. The girl I sewed Barbie clothes for and taught to bake chocolate chip cookies.

I cannot remember moving to reach her. I put my hand on her arm and rubbed the back of her shoulders. But I was not touching her. The years separated us.

Was it only last night that I had called to report her as a runaway? It seemed so long ago. . . .

WHERE
DID IT ALL BEGIN?

2

I CAN'T REMEMBER THE BEGINNING. Jill was always a self-willed little person. No Dr. Spock schedule for her; she made her own. From the word *Go* we seemed pitted against each other. I was determined to get her on our schedule; she was equally determined to run by her own clock. She would eat when it suited her. Before that, the strained peas would come spluttering back at me, and the bottle would be held without a suck. To detain her feeding, meant listening to bloodcurdling screams of protest. But when she was ready—ah! It must have been this intense need to do it her way that prompted her to eat with a spoon and drink from a cup before she was one.

Bedtime, too, became a battlefront. Not that she didn't want to go to bed. She just wanted to do it her own way. My way was to hold her lovingly and give her the last bottle of the day. When her eyes began to close drowsily, I would lay her gently in the crib. Her method was to scream hysterically for fifteen minutes, almost to the second. It seemed a harsh way to end the day. For months I would pick her up, but to no avail. I learned

19

that she would have her fifteen-minute squall regardless.

Dr. Spock was my guide. Didn't he say toilet training could be started when the baby sat up? Jill and I went that route with little or no success for almost a year. She seemed to be saying, "This is my thing, and I will do it when and where I choose." But on a hot summer day, clad only in tiny training pants, she went to the little chair herself. She earned the nickname "Puddles" before she became adept with stubborn buttons, but she did her own training.

Jill thrived on school. Here was something she could do at her own pace. She gave it her best and became overly involved.

One afternoon when Jill's first-grade class was studying Abraham Lincoln, she ran to the house crying. Her face was red; her eyes wild. She was sobbing so hard she could only choke in response to my anxious questions. After a long time, she gasped, "Mama, they killed Abraham Lincoln." In my relief, I cried with her: for Abraham Lincoln and for all mothers who worry about little girls.

During her adolescent years, Jill's timetable was always two jumps ahead of us. Many of her friends began to wear hose in the fifth or sixth grade. Never mind that they were full of runs and big holes or that they looked like little girls playing dress up. Jill was angry when we said junior high would be soon enough. But then the Girl Scout leader called and requested that Jill wear hose when the Scouts sang for a local service club. Sometimes it seemed the whole world was against me!

No matter what the issue or the reason, no matter what future day was set, Jill seemed determined to settle it sooner. There was the time we bought an electric shaver as a surprise for her thirteenth birthday. She had asked and asked for it; shaving was a status symbol among her friends. Finally giving it to her was a sign we recognized she was growing up. But before her birthday, I discovered telltale signs in the bathtub that she was already using her dad's razor. We never seemed able to give her anything.

Even when she had our permission, some inner force urged her to do more. When "everyone" was having their ears pierced, we agreed Jill could have hers done. The only stipulation was that a doctor do it, to guard against infection and scarring. On a visit to her cousin's, Jill had a homemade job done.

Setting any kind of curfew became an impossibility. No matter what time we set, she was a half hour or more late. Neither did allowing Jill to set her own guidelines work. Once agreed on, they became more rules to avoid.

I became increasingly agitated over our lack of control. *If we can't make her mind now, what will happen when she's older?* I kept thinking.

To me, Jill was a mystery, a living contrast. The friendships we tried to encourage became less than important. Instead, she made her own. When they included a boy who had already been in trouble with the police at fourteen and a girl whose older sister had to be married, we ran scared. But this same child gave her heart to a little boy with spina bifida and a deaf girl her own age who was shunned by others.

I became aware of Jill's sensitivity when she "adopted" Donna in the third grade. Donna was almost completely deaf. Although she was becoming adept at lip-reading,

21

one had to get Donna's attention and face her directly while talking. Jill assumed the role of advocate in the classroom, making certain Donna had "heard" all the instructions and gotten out the right materials to work with. Donna's speech—slow, drawled, difficult to understand—often became the object of jokes and mimicry. Jill sensed Donna's pain and determined to be her special friend.

When Jill was thirteen, she fell in love with Jimmy, a five-year-old victim of spina bifida, a defect of the spinal column, and a hydrocephalic. I was reluctant to have Jill baby-sit for him, feeling the responsibility of a child paralyzed from the waist down was too much for her. But she handled it with an expertise born out of caring. She would think up games he could play in his wheelchair; she taught him songs using hand motions. Once his little sister Debbie insisted Jill teach her to dance. As Jimmy watched the fun, he said, "Teach me to dance, too, Jill." Jill showed him how to move his hands, arms, and head in time to the music while she turned him in his chair.

Some of this same sensitivity led her to befriend others who knew rejection. Whether it was a child with the "wrong" color skin or one from the "wrong" part of town, Jill identified with their feelings of isolation. As I recognized this part of her, I was both proud and apprehensive. This sensitivity was a beautiful quality, but I wondered if she knew the difference between accepting persons and accepting their life-styles.

With a great deal of uneasiness, I watched Jill begin her first boy-girl relationship. Everything seemed to be "wrong" with Mike. I didn't know him. I only knew what I heard: He had been in trouble at school for fighting and truancy. At fourteen, he smoked and had a reputation for being drunk. Jill was able to move beyond his outward life-style and discover a person she could care for. I could not, or would not. The more I tried to hinder their relationship, the more determined Jill was to foster it.

When she was ready to enter the Lebanon Junior High School, she wanted to play in the marching band. Her forte was piano. But one does not carry an upright in a parade. That summer she asked for a flute. She went to band practice all those hot days with kids who had prior band experience. Hours were spent in her room blowing and blowing. Joe Haboush, the band instructor, saw her drive as a resource to be tapped, and that fall Jill was competing for first chair in the band's flute section.

If you had seen a picture of a group of girls, Jill wouldn't have stood out. She was average in the way of most young girls: long, squeaky-clean hair, handsomely proportioned features, and a sparkle in her eyes and turn to her mouth that bespoke health and ease. Her figure, once she attained puberty, was all that mine wasn't.

Jill was like a puppy on a leash, excited and eager to run free. Always pulling, she was willing to put up with the "choking." Meanwhile, I was holding on for dear life, feeling my arm being jerked out of its socket. Who's to blame for the struggle? The puppy, whose whole body pulsates with zest to explore the world? Or the trainer, wanting to protect the pup from cars, lostness, and other things that go bump in the night? Like the man and his dog, Jill and I didn't have the language to communicate.

TRAIN UP A CHILD

3

THERE IS NO DOUBT about it. I expected unquestioning obedience from my children. Like so many other persons in their mid-forties, I grew up in that kind of home. My father's word was law. We may not have liked it, we may have grumbled under our breath, but we did as we were told. Infractions of that law were met with swift, sure punishment. I can remember severe punishment being inflicted on my sister Hallie, a girl not unlike Jill—strong-willed and determined. I learned early to do exactly as I was told. So I grew up, became a mother, and expected my children to do the same. It's sad really, because I grew up quite afraid of my dad. And yet he was not a cruel man. He had learned to be a father from his heavy-handed stepfather and raised us the only way he knew.

I didn't want my four children to fear me or Gene. But even so, I began parenting the same way: slapping hands, swatting bottoms, and using a paddle toy on my kids for not eating their vegetables. As the children grew older and their offenses became worse, I found myself urging

Gene to be more firm. "If you would discipline them more, maybe they would learn," I told him. But Gene is a gentle, soft-spoken man. So I assumed the role of disciplinarian, feeling that somebody had to shape them up.

With the three boys, a hefty swat brought the results I expected: tears and, I thought, improved behavior. Jill was different. Her strong sense of self would not accept this kind of indignity. There were no tears, not even an "Ouch!" Just a glaring look and a firmer set to the chin. Instead of recognizing this as the wrong approach for this child, I increased the spankings. One day much later, she would tell her counselor that we hassled her more than the boys. It was true. The boys were "good," if *good* is to be interpreted as not rocking the boat.

She was hassled more and spanked more, until one day when Jill was going on eleven, I used a belt on her. It seemed so urgent that children learn to obey their parents. Jill lay across her bed and let me apply the strap. She did not cry. Suddenly, my anger vented, I became aware of the streaky, red welts on her little legs. I crossed the hall into my own room, and closing the door, leaned against it. The tears ran down my cheeks. I felt degraded, humiliated. I knew I would never use my hands on any of my children again. I never did. Later when Jill's problems were very real—no longer just a harmless part of growing up—I was glad Jill never again knew anything harsher than an angry voice.

It is strange how deeply ingrained an idea can become. Many times I questioned my new stance, wondering if my father's way was right. One day while talking to my mother about our inability to influence Jill, she said, "I'd just tell her. I'd *make* her mind!"

"How?" I asked. "By putting bars on her windows? By beating her? That doesn't work with Jill, and it makes me feel horrible."

"It's the way your dad and I raised you," she replied.

How could I explain that Jill wasn't the reason I left that method. It was for me. It did seem to be a workable solution for my parents. Perhaps it was a different time, or just different people.

Parents whose children are placid—who never make waves, who shape their wills to their parents' or do not seem to be in conflict with their parents' wishes—will react as my mother did. "I'd just *tell* them!" They do not know the mountain of words that go unheard. They do not know the consuming fear as some parents watch their child heading for disaster and are helpless to stop them.

Oh, I did *tell* her. Over and over again. Word upon word—warning words, pleading words, angry words, loving words, hurtful words . . . words . . . words . . . words. Words that just bounced back, because there was no one listening. I talked and talked while I watched my child backing farther and farther away. Moving towards all that I feared. Moving along the edge of a cliff, away from life and flirting with death. Not so much physical death as the death of her potential as a person.

SOMEWHERE
ALONG THE WAY

4

IN APRIL, 1970, THE LETTER came from the pulpit committee of the First Baptist Church of Evansville, Indiana. Was my husband interested in pursuing the possibilities of becoming their pastor?

We had talked to the children about such letters. "Someday," we had said, "a letter will come that will result in our moving." None of us wanted to think about it, but we knew it was true. Someday we would move from Lebanon.

It was such a good place to live, to raise a family, to grow up. Our roots were deep. Grandma Ton had moved here after grandpa died. Gene had taken part in community activities that gave him an identity beyond that of a pastor. The younger boys, Jeff and Joe, were active in Scouts and Little League. Jack had a part in the high school musical *Carousel*.

And Jill had a wide circle of friends in school and church. She had tried out for drum majorette with the junior high band, and we watched her prance down the street in the Fourth of July parade. She was elected to the

Junior High Honor Society. And, of course, there was Mike Campbell, her first boyfriend.

When we walked from the square up Washington Street and saw our church on the corner and our house next door, we felt at home.

We didn't tell the children about that first letter. Perhaps it was a mistake. In Baptist churches, the pastor's consideration of a move is supposed to be kept secret. So that whole summer while negotiations proceeded further, our children were unaware of the threat to their corner of the world. I guess we talked about the possibility of a move more often, but only in terms of someday.

In a few months we met the pulpit committee in Vincennes, a neutral territory where they could hear Gene preach. Some time later, he was asked to candidate for the position. That meant the committee would want to meet the whole family, so we had to tell the children.

All this culminated as we were ready to leave on vacation, so we planned to stop in Evansville overnight. After we were on the way—all six of us crowded into the car with our vacation gear—we explained all that had happened. There were no loud shouts of angry protest. Just a few quiet questions—"Is it for sure?" "When will we have to move?" Then there was a stillness rarely known when two adults and four children are packed into one vacation-bound sedan. Each of us drew inward to contemplate what this would mean to our own existence. Occasionally Gene or I broke the silence with some bit of information about our prospective home, either to bolster our own enthusiasm or to elicit some excitement from four suddenly solemn youngsters.

It was a disheartened family that trooped into the

Holiday Inn amidst a torrential downpour. Gene called Jim Waller, the chairman of the pulpit committee and our tour guide to the city. We met him at the arranged place and crawled into his station wagon. No city looks its best seen through windshield wipers. Evansville was no exception. Jim proudly showed us his town—the businesses, schools, two universities, our church, and the parsonage. But we saw everything compared to Lebanon. Evansville was sooooooooo big. This parsonage was so small compared to our huge older home in Lebanon. Harrison High School and Hebron didn't stand a chance, compared to Lebanon schools, filled with friends and memories of happy times.

The vacation in Gatlinburg, Tennessee, was miserable. We had planned on going there for such a long time. It was one of our first trips to anywhere besides grandma's. But even Jill and Jack were strangely silent, not bickering with each other once. Gene, firmly convinced he had arrived at the right decision for him, still hurt as he realized the pain he had brought to his family.

The big question was "When?" How soon would we have to move? Gene figured out the time needed to review the candidates and for the congregation to vote their acceptance. Then allowing for a month's notice, he arrived at the first part of October. Jack wondered about starting the school year in Evansville rather than beginning in Lebanon and having to transfer. We felt that could be arranged. Jill had no such wish. She would cling to every day left. She spent the days of our vacation in the motel room, writing letters home, withdrawn and morosely silent.

After returning to Lebanon, we prepared for the

weekend of candidating. I hate this aspect of being a pastor's wife. There's no gentler way to say it. Few other professions require that a man's entire family be on exhibition. Regardless of her husband's qualifications, a minister's wife soon learns she can make or break his opportunities. A handshake or a greeting can influence how people will vote. This time Jill and Jack would be under the same spotlight.

A parent does foolish things at a time like this. I encouraged Jack to get his hair cut, only to discover young people in Evansville wore theirs longer than he ever had. I reminded them over and over to be polite and responsive. But how do you sell yourself to a group of people when a part of you wishes they would vote no?

I do not pretend to understand what causes a man to move from one charge to another. Some term it "the call of God." I don't know about that, I have never been "called." But I do know what it is to lie next to a man as he tosses from side to side or lies wide-eyed, staring into the blackness. I know what it is to watch him worry that what he has chosen to do will hurt his family. My happiness is to be a part of that man's world, wherever it may be. But with each move, I enter into a period of grief and mourning. To walk through my empty home—checking it one last time after the movers have gone—to walk out the door for the last time is to cut myself off from a whole piece of my life. For all our differences, Jill and I share these feelings. As I watched her begin to pack, I knew what she was feeling. But there was one difference. I was committed to a man. My love for him and my desire to be the best wife I could gave me a reason for moving. In all my attempts to comfort Jill, I could not give her this.

Jeff and Joe quickly got caught up in the anticipation of moving. Jack was quiet; he was struggling to be grown-up and accept something very hard for him. Jill could not seem to cope. Perhaps it was her tremendous need to be self-directed that could not stand this one thing she couldn't manipulate. She did not express her anger verbally. Rather it was a set of her mouth and a look in her eyes. Her face was constantly red and puffy from crying, and soon broke out with a rash that covered a large part of her body.

The days of that last month went quickly. Friends dropped by to say good-bye. Others wrote notes of appreciation for our friendship. One father wrote a letter to the editor of the local newspaper, thanking Gene publicly for working with his sons in the Little League. There was even an editorial "The Impact of a Ton," in the evening paper. All these gestures affirmed and warmed us but they did not make leaving any easier.

Moving day dawned. Piece by piece our life in Lebanon was packed into a van. By the time the children came home from school, all but the last remnants were gone. I took my last walk through the now empty house. My footsteps echoed through rooms that had been filled with the sounds of a family living out their life together. It was like dying. "Life is a death-resurrection cycle," John Powell wrote in his book, *The Secret of Staying in Love.* "In every moment there is a death, a leaving what has been, and a birth, a stepping into what is and will be." A leaving behind and a moving toward, a little death and a new birth. As we waved good-bye to our friends, I saw only what I was leaving, and I wanted desperately to go back and claim what had been.

Darkness almost surrounded us as we drove out of town toward the highway. We had purchased an old car, which we named the "Red Baron." Jill, Jeff, and the gerbils rode in this car with me, Joe and our dog, Jock, with Gene. As we left the city on that rainy night, I realized I had not driven so far before. And the two children could not help. Behind us lay our home, our church, our friends—and ahead was only strangeness. My throat ached with the need to cry; but, you can't drive a car and cry.

Jeffrey was twelve that fall. He sat beside me, wide-eyed, prepared to help mother drive. At the time I had no idea how much that boy would help me in the years ahead.

Jill had immediately curled up in the backseat and cried herself to sleep. At first I felt angry. She was the oldest and should be helping me through this ordeal. Even then, I did not realize how deeply disturbed she was and how long the road "home" would be.

It was a long, lonesome trip that rainy October night. Neither Gene up ahead, nor I, following his red tail-lights, had any idea of the nightmare that awaited us. Somewhere on that road—somewhere between Lebanon and Evansville—we lost our daughter. It would be more than three years before she was able to find her way back to us.

IN AND OUT THE WINDOW

5

WHEN WE AWOKE IN EVANSVILLE the next morning, it was still raining. The kids half-jokingly asked, "Does it always rain in Evansville?" We decided to make a game out of their cynicism. For every "bad" about Evansville, we had to name two "goods." Although our "goods" sometimes seemed ridiculous, the game helped us focus on the here and now. I even made a banner with the words "Bloom where you are planted now" to hang in our family room.

Although I dislike tearing a home apart, I enjoy putting one together. So even though I was lonesome, I found pleasure in arranging our furniture to create a home that was attractive and livable. To my surprise, the house wasn't nearly as small as it had looked at first.

Gene and I tried to be sensitive to each other and to the adjustment the children were making. Jeff would have started junior high in Lebanon; here he was back in grade school. We tried to encourage him. "Just think, in two years you will be in high school and your Lebanon friends will still be in junior high." Jack was unable to join any of the musical groups at the high school, something he had enjoyed in Lebanon. But he did get into the church's production of the musical *Life*.

Neither Jeff nor Joe ever found Scout troops that they felt a part of. And when summer came, they lost out in Babe Ruth and Little League tryouts to players who had grown up on the local teams. The boys had their share of disappointments and frustrations, but they seemed to be willing to overlook them. Maybe that's why Jill's inability to handle the change seemed more stubbornness than anything else.

When Jill curled up on the backseat during our trip to Evansville, it was the beginning of a systematic withdrawal.

I did not realize until later how she viewed these early days. Whereas the new house now looked larger to me, to Jill it was still small and ugly. Years later, she recalled her feelings. . . .

"I felt there was only one good room in the whole house—Jack's bedroom. It was paneled in cherry. My room in the old house was light pink, and mom had painted all my furniture a darker pink. The carpet had pink roses on it. It was the neatest room I had ever had. And now this ugly green room would be mine. Mom said it could be painted any color I wanted, but I didn't care. I hated it. There was yukky linoleum in the kitchen. It was all torn up. And the family room downstairs stunk; it smelled. Our bathroom at home was all shades of grey ceramic tile and had a glassed-in shower with sliding doors. This one didn't even have a shower. There was one in my folks' room. But I knew they wouldn't let all four of us run through there to use it."

42

These were only the outward inconveniences that might have changed with time. But Jill's reaction to the new school never seemed to change. . . .

"I really dreaded going that first day. I remember what I wore—my brown-checked skirt, brown sweater, and knee socks. I was scared to death. There were so many people. All the faces coming toward me in the hall seemed like a nightmare. Not a familiar one in the crowd. Surrounded by all those people, I felt isolated—all alone and sure everyone was looking at me and laughing.

"It was so different. In Lebanon the new girl was something special. All the girls talked about how cute she was, and the boys wanted to take her out. Everyone tried to get her in their group at lunch and after school. Here, nobody paid any attention to you at all. No one even spoke. You made your own way, or you didn't make it.

"Every class meant another roomful of strangers. Glee club was the only one I liked. We rang bells, and a few of the girls talked to me. But it wasn't the same. They sang dumb music—duddy songs. In Lebanon, I had been the glee club pianist—someone special.

"I felt so ugly. Everyone had pretty clothes and nice cars. They didn't nickname Harrison kids 'cake eaters' for nothing. We were out of our league in the neighborhood and at school.

"Then I began to put on a lot of weight. That didn't help. I was really ugly then. I didn't have nice clothes, and I was fat, too. Besides that, the rash that had started before we moved wouldn't go away. My face was all red and cracked. The doctor prescribed some stuff to put on it, but it wouldn't clear up. It was on my arms and neck too, but that didn't matter. If only my face hadn't looked

43

so ugly and blotchy, maybe I could have . . .

"For a long time I felt sick every morning. I hated getting up and going to school. I dreaded going into the lunchroom by myself and having to stand in line alone and find a place to sit. Everyone else had someone to be with. I think I'd have died if I had known that strangeness would last into my senior year. . . ."

Jill shut herself into her room for longer and longer periods of time. After a while, she left it only to go out or to eat her meals. Sometimes she would emerge to practice the piano, the only part of her old self that remained. She would not try out for the school band. The handbell choir lured her for a short time, but then she dropped out, saying they used dumb music. So we made a down payment on a piano and encouraged her to continue lessons. Her teacher was knowledgeable and strict, one who would demand Jill's best. Once she would have thrived on that kind of challenge. Now she only complained about us making her take lessons. At the same time, she seemed proud of her increasing skill and her ability to merit a high score in an audition before the Guild of Piano Artists. Shortly after the audition, however, she just quit. There was no making her; she simply would not go back.

Jill had been gregarious by nature, having many close friends. She had derived real pleasure out of being with them, talking on the phone and writing long notes. Now she seemed to refuse to make friends. Did she think the risk was too great? The hurt too deep? There were only a few girls she called friends. As for boys, well, she was not about to like any boy here. At first they had asked her out. But she sat them down hard, and few called back.

The word got around that she wasn't interested. She did agree to go with one of the boys from our church to his junior prom. Afterwards she wanted to renege, but we insisted she go. They were both miserable: he had wanted to go with another girl, and she hadn't wanted to go at all.

Jill liked Mike. It was as simple as that; except Mike was in Lebanon, and Jill was here. Gene and I had been relieved to move away from him. But Jill clung tenaciously to that friendship. Every day she wrote long letters to Mike and her other friends back "home." And every day she received mail in return. In this way, she kept alive all the old friendships and didn't seem to need new ones here.

It was almost as if it would be a sign of giving up if she enjoyed anything about Evansville. She would not like the school, the church, or the people in it.

Her bedroom became her fortress; her three brothers, her father, and I, the enemy. The mess in her room seemed to become a symbol of her inner confusion and turmoil. Rotten apple cores, dirty glasses, torn papers, cylinders from tampons, soiled underwear, and shed clothes littered the floor and beds. She kept the shades down most of the time and let the lights burn even when she was gone.

Jill felt hassled. I suppose she was. The accumulation of filth in her room irritated me. Consciously or unconsciously, I believe it was her way to hassle me. She seemed to do everything she could to annoy or frustrate us. If the heat was on, she would open her windows. If we asked her to turn off the lights, she went out leaving them on, and her radio besides. Not so the radio could be heard—

45

just on. When I asked her to put her dirty clothes in the hamper on wash day, she waited until the next day and then ran one pair of jeans through the entire wash and dry cycle. When I tried to explain that the soap, water, and electricity cost money, she gave me her Whew!-you-make-a-case-out-of-everything expression, or said, "I needed them. Everything's dirty."

The money was important, but not crucial. The real irritation was that this child boldly defied us, and we were helpless to do anything about it.

Once in the very beginning, a glimmer of the old Jill broke through. In our denomination, when a family moves, it is customary to join the new church by walking forward at the end of the worship service. It was assumed that we would do this on our first Sunday in Evansville. Knowing that this church was not of their choosing, we suggested Jill and Jack wait until they honestly wanted to be members. So on the morning Gene and I joined the church, Jack went forward with us. Jill stayed in the pew. At lunch that day, we affirmed her decision. About a month later, she came down the aisle herself and asked for membership. For just that few minutes, she was smiling and happy, looking almost free. Then, just as quickly, she put herself back into her box.

By bits and pieces, we began to learn what her adopted life-style was to be—a chance remark, little things that didn't make sense. Finally, through our own checking, we uncovered lie after lie. I might have understood if there had been any real reason for it, but most of the time there wasn't. She would lie about where she was going, even though we had given her permission to go there. She seemed to want to see if she could get away with it.

One day I found a pile of cigarette butts outside her window. When I confronted her with them, she said she hadn't put them there; and furthermore she didn't smoke.

Later Gene and I noticed that her screen was loose. As we worked to replace it, we saw it had been pried out in one corner. That was how we discovered Jill had been using her bedroom window to escape. She came and went without our knowledge, and often left after we were in bed. Sometimes she just went out and wandered in the woods near our home or spent the night on our patio. I often stood outside her door, holding my breath, just listening for some sound to tell me she was in there.

In the beginning, I tried to accept Jill's feelings of resentment. I knew she was lonely and angry; I tried to share my own feelings of loneliness and separation. But her response was always, "You have daddy." It accomplished nothing to remind her that she had him, too, or to say that we were a family and could help each other. If I said the boys were making the adjustment because they were willing to reach out and make new friends, she only resented the comparison. I tried teasing her out of her depression by singing the Brownie song we had learned together about making new friends and keeping the old. After awhile, I gave up.

A part of her wanted to strike back. She knew where we were most vulnerable and staged her attack by balking at going to our church. She referred to the church where she had a job playing the organ as "my church." That hurt. But if she had found a place there, good! She accepted an office in our youth group and then didn't want to go anymore. We told her she had accepted the responsibility and would have to go, or resign. She went grudgingly, angrily, but would not resign.

I did not understand what was happening. I didn't know her anymore. Her language changed, even the sound of her voice. But the most observable difference was in her face: it became sullen and hard looking. The farther she withdrew from us, the tighter I tried to hold on. Her unpredictable behavior scared me. I could not trust her. My stomach had tightened into a knot that seldom went away.

If only Jill could have told me how she was feeling, if only I could have reached her. Not until our nightmare was over did she explain. . . .

"I felt terrible about myself. In Lebanon I could do things—be in the band, play the piano, be a majorette. I had friends. I was skinny. Here I was just a dumb, fat, clumsy klutz.

"Then some weird things started to happen. My speech got all slurred. My tongue felt rubbery and too big for my mouth. It wouldn't move the way I wanted it to. I lost some visual perception and walked into walls. Once I fell all the way down the stairs. Even my handwriting got funny. Mom and dad sent me to the doctor, but he said there wasn't anything wrong.

"It felt good to sleep. I wanted to sleep and sleep and never wake up. When I was awake, I daydreamed. In my mind, I was going back to Lebanon to see Mike and my friends; I played the scene a thousand different ways. It was a wonder my grades stayed so good, because even at school I was in a fantasy world. At home, I sat at my window or took long walks in the woods nearby. Many times I would wander up there in the middle of the night.

My folks cautioned me about that, but I couldn't see any harm in it. The little wooded area became my hideaway. I felt peaceful there, listening to the wind in the trees.

"In a way, it was like drowning. I just floundered around. In Lebanon I felt put together, like my world was in order. I knew what I wanted. In Evansville, I had no goals, nothing I wanted—except to return to Lebanon."

AN EMPTY BED

6

IT IS UNCANNY how a particular sight or sound can send one spiraling backward in time. For a brief instant, it is as though we relive a moment in our past. This happens to Grandma Ton even now in the wee hours of the morning when she gets up to go to the bathroom. Her eyes glance at the door to the spare bedroom, and she feels the shock of seeing a bed that is empty when it's supposed to be occupied. She relives the panic of not knowing where her granddaughter has gone. . . .

We had not meant to involve Gene's mother in our problems with Jill. But the first summer after we moved to Evansville, grandma asked Jill to go with her to Colorado. It seemed like such a good idea. Grandma would have company on a long trip, and Jill and the rest of us would have a respite from the hostility that was part of everyday and almost every conversation.

So they made the trip west together. On the way home,

they stopped at grandma's house in Lebanon. I think Jill endured the whole trip just to get back there. Grandma was determined to keep her away from some of her friends who seemed to be a bad influence. She arranged for Jill to have lunch with Karen, a young woman who had experienced the same problems in her teenage years. I suspect grandma expected Karen to set Jill straight.

After lunch, Jill went to the municipal pool, where everyone gathers in the summer. When Grandma Ton went to pick her up, Jill was gone.

She called Jill's best friend Carla, knowing Jill would be there, and told her to "get." Grandma blamed Carla for some of our trouble with Jill, and she was upset to find her there. Nor did it help that Mike brought Jill back to the house.

Later, when Jill asked if she might spend the night with Carla, grandma answered an emphatic no. The two of them watched tv until ten o'clock and went to bed.

About 5:00 A.M., grandma woke up and went into the hall. Jill's door was open, and it had been closed the night before. Even before she saw the empty bed, she was alarmed.

For a while she just sat in a chair in the living room trying to collect her thoughts. She knew now that Jill had used her to get back to Lebanon. But where had Jill gone and why? She checked to see what was missing. Not much: a pair of old jeans, a top, her makeup bag. About six o'clock she called our good friends the Larrs. They both came at once.

George and Margaret Larrs felt close to Jill, as they did to all our children and we did to theirs. Mike, Deb, and

Pat were the same ages as our kids, and our families had enjoyed many good times together. To our four, George and Margaret were Mama and Papa Larrs. George owned the International Harvester dealership in Lebanon. Margaret was his bookkeeper, and I had worked for both of them for almost five years. Margaret and I had talked a lot about our children's prcblems; it seemed to help keep things in perspective.

Just the summer before, Jill had been on a church retreat with them. Jill had told Margaret how badly she felt about moving but said she understood it was part of her dad's job. Jill walked in her sleep, particularly when she was upset. That night she had walked right off the top bunk, and Margaret had nursed her smashed face.

As George and Margaret arrived at Grandma Ton's, they tried to decide how to find Jill. But first, they wanted to call us.

We had just gotten up when the phone rang. We listened as a frightened grandmother told us the story. To us, it sounded like a bunch of unconnected pieces. What was Jill doing? Where was she? Why would she do this to her grandmother?

As we headed for Lebanon, I tried to control my feelings—the too-full, nauseated ache in my stomach, the trembling hands, the fear. Like the first time you try to walk after an operation. You know you won't be able to make it; but you do.

Quite suddenly I realized I was afraid to find her, to face her. At the same time, I wondered how I could live if we didn't. What do you say to your sixteen-year-old daughter who has run away? There in the car, speeding down the highway, I rehearsed. I thought of all the right things to say—like it says in the books. Instead, all the garbage started to come out.

That was the first time. Every other time is the same. It is not something you "adjust" to.

Lebanon was such a small town that it was not difficult to find Jill, just frustrating. The teenagers who knew about Jill's disappearance tried to protect her. After George had failed to get information from Carla or Denise, another friend of Jill's, he contacted a policeman he knew and persuaded him to question Carla further. Seeing the uniform, Carla admitted she had taken Jill to the Carr's, a home where the parents were out of town for the weekend.

George had been to this home earlier. But the boys had said Jill wasn't there. Now George and the policeman returned. Knowing that Carla had taken Jill there, the policeman pressed harder, and Jill finally came to the door. It didn't take much persuasion for George to convince her to come to his house.

When George returned to Grandma Ton's, Gene, the boys, and I had just arrived. He had spent six hours tracking down leads. We gathered around the kitchen table to hear his story.

Now that Jill was found, my concern evaporated, and I was angry and humiliated.

"If she doesn't want to live with us, then just let her stay here," I shouted.

George tried to deal with my anger, telling me Jill would probably be fine once we got back home. I didn't feel he, or anyone else, understood just how bad things really were.

Gene went with George to get Jill. I waited. I didn't

want to see her. When they returned, I tightened up inside, as though to protect myself. I threw up some barriers of my own that day, and together we began the construction of a wall. That wall would grow into a monstrous bulwark before the end of it.

HOW TO BUILD A WALL

7

IT WAS A LONG RIDE from Lebanon to Evansville. The two little boys sat stiff and unnaturally quiet. Jill was asleep or pretending to be. Gene and I must have churned a million thoughts over in our minds: The predominant question was "Now what?"

The boys, wondering what we might do next, waited, probably expecting the worst. Jill did, too. It was our move. But, we had no idea what to do or say. All we knew was that our child had tried to run away. She wanted no part of us. We were hurt by her rejection. And we were angry. A problem that had been a private matter was now exposed for all to see. We were plainly perplexed. What would *she* do now?

I was determined to be prepared for whatever might happen. So I began to search her room, reading everything I found. I read all her letters and every note from school. I went through her drawers, not even knowing what I was after. If she left a letter out on her desk to finish, I read that, too. I knew every time a letter came, because I brought in the mail. Sometimes I steamed them open; other times I waited for the first chance to search for them.

From all that I read, I learned Jill fantasied a lot. She wrote things that could not have taken place. I discovered that she not only lied to us, but she lied to her friends about what we were doing to her. Her language shocked me. There was a part of me that hated what I was doing. But I couldn't stop. What was happening to me? Like an alcoholic, I went to her room in secret and drank and drank.

And of course, Jill knew what I was doing. . . .

"At first, I couldn't believe mom was snooping around in my room. I just never thought she would do that; I figured she must have been looking for something. When I realized she was reading all my stuff, it made me mad. She always talked about respecting other people's property! It embarrassed me, too. So much of what I wrote wasn't true; I didn't want anyone to see it. Yet the bigger the story I could write or tell her, the better. If it was shocking, better still. I made up some weird stuff. I was tired of the image of the 'P.K.'—the pastor's kid. It became a big thing to do something my folks thought wrong.

"If I tried smoking, drinking, or staying out late, I could be 'in' with the kids I wanted to be friends with. Once I thought I knew who I was. Now I wasn't sure.

"A long time later, my friend David said, 'Jill, I have watched you wear a thousand masks, trying to be so many different people. But I always knew the real Jill. . . .' "

It was from reading Jill's letters that I learned Mike had been at summer camp. This had been a hard decision for us to make. Before Jill ran away, we had promised she could go to church camp with her friends from Lebanon. But we had dreaded her going back. Maybe her punishment should have been no camp. However, we felt that would only increase her hostility.

Now I realized that Jill and Mike had spent a great deal of time together. I have no idea how he got on the grounds and managed to be around. What I read led me to believe that my little girl was no more. Her innocence was far behind her.

Something seemed to snap inside me. Knowing how much she "made things up," I hoped I was wrong. If I wasn't, I didn't want to know any more. But having once begun, my appetite was insatiable. I, who had taught my children to respect others' privacy, now violated this most personal corner of Jill's life.

Because we could scarcely talk to one another, I began writing her notes. When I did try to talk with her, she would sit—her head bent, her eyes downcast—acting as if she didn't hear me. I would go on and on, until my voice choked up and I could go no farther. I wrote notes, asking her to do some chore, telling her something she needed to know, or, on rare occasions, trying to say "I love you in spite of all this." When I found out that she mocked my crying in her letters and made fun of my notes, I gave up trying to communicate at all. I felt like she stomped on me every time I reached out.

Something was growing inside me, getting bigger and bigger, filling me up and taking control: guilt. Guilt at what I was becoming—a prying, angry person, a mother who could not love her own child the way she needed to be loved. I began to feel responsible for what Jill was becoming. Over and over I asked the same question:

Where did I fail her? What should I have done differently? And the biggest one: Why does God let this happen?

At the end of the summer, two events helped Gene and me to relax a little. First, Mr. Haboush, Jill's band teacher from Lebanon, stopped to see her. Jill had written him occasionally, and sometimes he would answer her letters. For a few minutes, as she stood in the driveway visiting with him, she seemed like her old self. Gene and I were touched that he had taken the time to come see her.

The second was when we discovered Mike had broken up with Jill. He said it was stupid for them to keep going together if it kept her so stirred up. Now we hoped Jill would make some friends in Evansville.

But our joy was short-lived. Feeling sorry for Jill, Carla talked another boy in Lebanon into writing her. And the letters began to come every day, from someone I didn't know and Jill barely did.

One day this boy, Eddie, showed up in Evansville. He and some friends were camping nearby for a night or two. Jill wanted to take a sleeping bag and join him. For reasons that were obvious to us, we said no. But she couldn't understand why, and we wondered if she would obey us. Ever since we discovered her window was her escape hatch, we never knew if she was in her room or not. Once again I found myself in the hall outside her door, listening for some sound. Was she in there? I could have just opened her door and walked in. Why didn't I? Maybe I didn't want to know the truth.

Every day the mail brought a letter from Eddie, sometimes more than one. From things he wrote and from people we knew in Lebanon, we learned he was using drugs. Everything I had ever read about drugs came to haunt me. Up to now, this had all seemed like a bad dream. Sooner or later, we'd wake up, and it would be over. Now it became a nightmare. I read a letter from him urging her to let him get her "something." It would help her cope, he said. He told her about his own use of· drugs and described his trips. To me it was like something from a cheap magazine. I had never dreamed this could happen to my own family.

There were times now when Jill lied about baby-sitting. Either she hadn't been there at all, or had been earlier, but wasn't now. One night I woke up at one-thirty. Sensing that she hadn't come home yet, I checked her room. At three-thirty, I called the house where she was supposed to be baby-sitting. A sleepy voice told me, "She isn't here. She left with Eddie about twelve-thirty." I hadn't known he was in town.

It frightened me to know he had been there. I had read a story once about a young girl tripped out on acid by her friends while she was baby-sitting. Every detail tumbled through my mind that night. In the morning, I forbade Jill ever to baby-sit again. I told her I was horrified to know she had taken Eddie there. I could scarcely believe Jill had made those children vulnerable to that kind of danger. But the most astounding thing of all was that it made no difference to their mother. She would have continued to use Jill for a sitter if I had not refused. In a way, I understand. It was hard enough for me to grasp the sordidness Jill was involved in. How could I expect anyone else to see it as anything but a wild story?

I wanted to shake her, to pound her, rarely, to love her. But more often, I just wanted to get rid of her. I wanted out of all this. She was ruining *my* home, disrupting *my* life, and flaunting all *my* values. I couldn't reach out to her anymore. My own needs engulfed me, and I was lost.

As time went by, I could see physical changes in Eddie. His eyes became dull and listless, like a child's with a fever. His posture and carriage became increasingly indolent, and finally his speech seemed hesitating and slurred. I had such mixed emotions for this boy. Sometimes I hated him and wished him dead and away from my daughter. At other times, I cried for him. I wondered what manner of hell his parents were going through. I ached for them and for all parents who watched their children die in this way—slowly, willfully working at their own destruction.

Christmas, 1971, came and went. Our second Christmas in Evansville. It was cold, but the temperature had nothing to do with it. Jill refused to have any part in the traditional family observances. Ever since the children were small, we had lit Advent candles, read favorite Christmas stories, listened to recordings of familiar carols, and gone to special church services—always together. With Jill sulking in her bedroom, all that changed. We went through the appropriate motions, but the joy was gone. Doing dishes one night, I remembered a very little girl sitting close beside me as we turned the pages of the storybook and listened to *Amahl and the Night Visitors*. Sometimes we listened to this same record when she was home from school sick. How I wished I had that little girl back again. The fervor of that wish brought tears, and the tears brought anger, pain, and bitterness. I needed Christ to be reborn in me that year. But the fullness of time had not yet come.

LIKE A SHOOTING STAR

8

SOON AFTER CHRISTMAS, the phenomenon known as the Junior Jollies took place. Jill had shown no interest in any of Harrison High School's activities. Suddenly, she announced that she and a few friends were going to participate in the Junior Jollies. This was an annual event to earn money for the junior prom. Some of the juniors displayed their talents; others, their sillies. Jill and her friends went "silly." The preparations for this event excited her. To us, it was like a shooting star—appearing out of nowhere and bursting into light.

The girls planned their costumes carefully, and we helped Jill collect the paraphernalia she needed. She borrowed big, old tennis shoes from Jeff, bib overalls from Jack, and a plaid flannel shirt from her dad. Since she needed assistance getting in and out of the getup, we all helped. The neck of the shirt was buttoned around her waist. Then the overalls were put on around her hips, with the legs rolled up, so some of her striped knee socks showed. The overall straps were fastened to the shoulders of the shirt with safety pins. And the shirtsleeves were carefully tucked into the overall pockets. A pillow case—with eyes cut out and a silly face—was pulled down over her head and arms and tucked into the neck of the shirt at her waist. Voila! A comical little character ready to dance. And dance Jill did—up and down the hallway. The more we laughed, the goofier she got, as though all her bottled-up fun was coming out at one time.

A few weeks later, she told us she had decided to ask David to take her to the prom. A really nice boy, David had been a good friend of Jill's in Lebanon. We were ecstatic. We had never dreamed she would go with anyone but Eddie.

One day she asked me to go look at a dress she had seen in a store window. This was a real occurrence since we never went anywhere together. Still our tastes were so different, I was half afraid to see it. But the gown was beautiful. It was made of muslin and circled with antique lace that was interwoven with ribbon and embroidered trim. Besides being pretty and feminine, it was too expensive. Suddenly, I was tense, knowing there would be another battle.

But then she asked, "Mom, could you make one just like it?"

I used to make her clothes when she was younger. Lately, anything I made hung unworn, in her closet. I was pleased that she asked me to make this dress with such confidence.

"Yes, Jill, I think I can," I answered.

Nothing could have prevented me from producing that dress. Jill and I shopped until we found a similar pattern. We unearthed gobs of lace my mother had sent us a long time ago. Working with different brews of tea,

70

we experimented until we found just the right shade to dye the lace the same antique color. When the dress was finished, it looked exactly like the one in the window. Jill tried it on. She looked beautiful, almost radiant—if only she had smiled.

Gene and I would be out of town the night of the prom, but Grandma Ton was coming to stay. A day or so before we left, Jill modeled her dress, so her dad could take some pictures. That night, her grandmother took some more. We laugh at those pictures now; they illustrate that invisible wall. In Gene's pictures, Jill is scowling at the camera. But in grandma's, she is smiling happily as she holds David's arm. With us gone, she could relax and enjoy the evening.

At first, I had been disappointed at Jill's lack of enthusiasm for the dress when it was finished. But when Gene and I saw Grandma Ton's pictures, I knew she was pleased. That was enough.

For a brief span of time we had known laughter and happiness. But like a shooting star, the moments passed so quickly and completely that I wondered if they had been imagined.

Before long, Jill began talking more and more about going back to spend her senior year in Lebanon and graduate with "her" class. Once we might have considered that, but not now. We didn't know what her problem was, but we were certain it went much deeper than our move.

However, we did make some phone calls to see if she could do this on her own volition. She didn't want to believe what we found out: she would need a legal guardian there. Jill knew she had spoiled her chances of her

71

grandmother's accepting that responsibility. She also knew that if she felt hassled at home, it would be worse at grandma's. Somehow she maneuvered Carla's parents into assuming the guardianship. At least the girls said so. But it seemed inconceivable to us to sign our daughter over to someone we didn't know. Despite our negative response, Jill continued to insist that this was one thing she would do.

I dreaded the day school would be out. Summer meant long hours of having Jill around the house. The more time we spent together, the wider the separation seemed to become. We argued constantly—over her ironing piled up in the laundry room, over the talcum powder she applied in front of her bedroom door and then walked into the hall carpet, over the hours she spent lying in her bed or talking on the telephone. Everything, big and small, became another brick in the wall between us. We couldn't talk about the simplest things. How could we break through on the big ones?

But what was big? My objectivity had become clouded by fear and suspicion. Little things were magnified, and major issues loomed to gargantuan proportions. I was so afraid. Afraid Eddie would persuade her to use drugs. Worse still was she already on them? Wouldn't that explain her crazy behavior? With just her senior year left, I was afraid we couldn't keep her at home and in school long enough to graduate.

Long before now, I had urged her to use the pill. It was hard to do, so against everything I believed in. But to have ignored the possibility of pregnancy would have been foolish. So one day I had told her, in effect, if you can't be what we want you to be, then please use the pill.

Her only response was a cold, silent stare. To this day, I don't know if I told her that to hurt her—to say, "I believe this about you"—or to protect her. My biggest fear was that she would fall over the edge, that she would make an irrevocable mistake.

If lying and ignoring our wishes were her weapons, then silence became one of mine. We would pass each other on the stairs, and I would act as though she weren't there. We would sit at the table, share the same room— the same house—for a whole day, and I would not speak to her. A part of me knew how wrong this was. But I didn't care. She was hurting me, and I would hurt back. So, instead of verbal hostility, it became an inward thing, cold and ominous and strangling the life out of both of us.

Soon I was angry at everyone. My husband, so gentle and caring, would sit on the edge of the bed, stroking my hand and wanting to make the hurt disappear. My sobbing came from some place deep within and even sounded frightening to me. Yet, as he tried to comfort me, I was angry at him. I wanted him to have an answer. I wanted him to solve the problem. He didn't. He couldn't. If he could counsel others, why not us?

The boys felt my anger, too. Didn't they know all the grief we had? Didn't they care? How could they keep on jawing at each other or being so silly? How could they ask for a pair of jeans that wasn't ironed or a shirt that wasn't washed? Yet if I couldn't even keep the washing and ironing done, I really was a failure as a mother.

And what about our church? Wasn't the church supposed to be a caring community? Where were they now? I went on Sunday mornings; I smiled and said, "Good morning, how are you today? Oh, sure, I can give a book report for you."

Why didn't they leave me alone? I couldn't even cope with the washing. I was asked to give an inspirational talk. What a joke. I kept thinking it was their fault we were here. Maybe if we'd stayed in Lebanon none of this would have happened. There were Sundays when I wanted to stand up and holler, "Help! Don't you know? Don't you care? I'm dying inside."

I felt haunted by a sadness for all that had been. Where had I lost her? Where were we when we got separated? Now I can't even find her; that child who was born on a cold March morning. Even then I was happy she was a girl. I would sew dresses for her, and she would stand on a chair and dry dishes with me. I would show her how to make paper dolls and little ladies out of hollyhocks. And when she got older, we would have long talks about menstruation and boys and sex. She would not come to it as I had. I would send for one of those kits advertised in the magazines. Boys are nice, but they're for their dads. Girls are for moms. Now we lived in the same house and never touched.

Sometimes I wondered who was lost, Jill or me? I felt like I had once years ago when my mother took me shopping. One minute she was there at my side and the next—only strangers. I couldn't see her. I remember thinking I was going to throw up. All those people hurrying around me, yet I felt so alone. Now, surrounded by persons who loved and cared about me—Gene, my boys, our church family—I was alone again.

Where was God? Why would he let this happen? I believed I was being punished for no reason. I had been a

74

good mother. Jill had been loved. She had been brought up in a Christian home, taken to church and church school. Her parents loved each other. I did all the things a good mother was supposed to do. I took my turn as room mother, led her Girl Scout troop, read to her, played with her. Why hadn't it worked? Didn't the Bible promise "Train up a child in the way he should go, and when he is old he will not depart from it?" Bunk! If that was a lie, maybe it was all a lie. . . . No! I couldn't hate a vacuum as I now hated God. He was real, all right. But where was the guidance and peace he promised?

THE BEST AND THE WORST

9

THE SUMMER OF '72 was a paradox. To say it was the worst of summers would be true. To say it was the best would also be true. It was both the end of the road and the way out—an ending and a beginning.

Even roads that seem to be going in only one direction eventually turn. Sometimes the bend is so slight, the curve so gradual, that we don't realize we have changed direction. That's how it was that summer.

Early in August, Jeffrey went to Indian Creek Baptist Camp. What happened to him there was to influence our entire family.

Jeff was shy and sensitive. He often came out on the short end because of it. He was a person who would rather switch than fight. In a family of four youngsters, that often meant going someone else's way. We would tell him, "You don't always have to back down." But with a slight shrug of his shoulders, he would walk away. Most of the time, the issue just wasn't important enough to him.

He is also the kind of guy whose eyes fill suddenly with tears when he knows someone is hurting—a tender, beautiful quality in any person, but doubly rich in a man. Because he was sensitive and open, he was ready to respond when God touched him that summer at camp. It was a turning point for him—a bend in his road that turned toward God.

I will never forget the day he returned. Even after he had put his gear away, he hung around the house, nervous and fidgety. Like most mothers, I was on the move. When I finally lit on the couch in the front room to read, he came and sat in the blue chair. He was rocking too hard, and I was just on the verge of telling him so. Back and forth, back and forth. He knew that chair tipped over easily, and I was getting irritated.

Then he began to talk about the week at camp, becoming more excited as he went along. I began to sense that something had happened to him. Putting down the newspaper, I looked at him. His cheeks were bright pink; his eyes sparkled. "Mom," he said, "I didn't know it could be like that. I didn't know God could be so real."

He talked about the consecration service, the campfire, and the love these teenagers felt for God and each other as they shared this mountaintop experience. He had been through it all before, but never quite like this.

And now, listening to him, I felt that same touch. I knew God was reaching out to me, for I had felt his touch before, long ago. Something familiar stirred within me, like a name you know well but can't recall. Slowly at first, and then more and more clearly, I realized that Jeff was *God's* child. Given into my care for a brief time, but God's child still. A person, complete, apart from me. God was acting in his life without my help.

It was a long time before I realized the impact of what had happened to me. Falling with a domino-like effect, the Spirit of God finally reached not only my relationship with Jill but with the boys as well.

It was a gentle, touching moment in the middle of a harsh, abrasive summer, and for a few days it acted as a soothing ointment, dulling the hurt.

But our sore had festered long enough. One summer evening, it opened. The rupture was ugly and awful, but necessary for healing.

In order to understand what happened that night, you need to visualize our neighborhood. Our house is one of four homes on a short boulevard that leads to a cul-de-sac. Beyond lies a big wooded area and then a hill topped by some big homes that face Newburgh Road. Jill often walked these woods in the middle of the night.

As Gene, Jack, and I sat talking in the living room that night, we saw the lights of a car pulling onto the boulevard and up into the cul-de-sac. In a little while, Jill came in and went to her room. The car did not leave. Jack went outside, through the neighbor's backyard, and returned to report the car was Eddie's. He was sitting there, as though he were waiting.

Our nerve ends were raw. Why didn't Eddie leave? What was he waiting for? I wanted Gene to tell him to go. But he said Eddie, or anybody else, could park there if they wanted to. We couldn't tell him to leave just because he made us uncomfortable.

About then, I saw someone move past our front windows. Gene went to the door just in time to see Jill run into the cul-de-sac and disappear.

"Jill, Jill, come back!" Gene called.

We stood there, stunned, feeling frightened and angry. Too confused to think what to do next. Then Eddie's car started, and we watched it pull back onto the boulevard across from our house.

"She's in his car. I know she's in that car," I screamed. "Make him stop and get her out of there."

Gene ran across the median toward the car. Eddie stopped and got out. Now I was afraid of what he might do. Pictures of things I had read about kids on drugs raced through my mind. Gene could see that Jill was not in the car.

"Make him open the trunk. She probably crawled into the trunk." My voice seemed eerie and unreal.

Eddie would not unlock the trunk. He said he didn't have a key. Both of us were afraid to push him too far. He got back in his car, pulled onto Washington Street, and was gone.

I was shaking all over as we came back into the house. I simply could not control my body.

"I'm going to call the police," I said and headed into our bedroom, picking up the phone book as I went. Gene wanted me to stop a minute.

"Take a little time to calm down," he said. "Let's try to collect ourselves and sort this through."

"No. I've done what you thought long enough. We have to stop her—before it's too late."

I wonder how many times a night that policeman answers the phone to have some hysterical mother tell him her daughter has run away. Very matter-of-factly, he asked how old she was.

"Seventeen."

He told me how many kids run away every night.

Not my daughter, I thought.

"Wait until morning and see if she doesn't come home by herself. If we pick her up, she will have a juvenile record, and you'll have to come get her."

"I want her picked up. Of course, we'll come get her."

"Call back in the morning, lady."

We lay awake watching the hands of the clock go around, waiting for the sound of the front door. Bodies tense, every muscle taut, we listened to every noise—every creak of the house, every click as the air conditioner turned on and off and every car that passed in the night. One o'clock. Two o'clock. Three.

We had played this scene before, waiting for her to come home—listening and waiting. *Check her room . . . maybe you dosed for just a minute and she came back . . . no.* Even her empty bedroom seemed odd as we looked in.

Morning came as it always does. The sun was shining. Funny how the days seemed the same.

Now the crucial question had to be answered. Should I call the police? Somehow it sounded cruel. *If they do find her, she'll have a juvenile record. Do I want to do that to her? And what about Gene and me? What will it mean to us? Will we have to go to court? Will we be judged unfit parents? Not Gene, surely.* He had been so kind to her—trusting her when it seemed utterly ludicrous to me, trying to reach her long after I had given up. If anyone was unfit, it was me. In some way, all of this was my fault. I was guilty.

But what if they don't find her? What then? What will become

83

of her? Where will she go? What will she be doing? I dialed the number very slowly and deliberately.

Then I wandered listlessly through the house. Gene left for the church office to finish some work. Tomorrow was Sunday, and some three hundred people would gather to hear his sermon. I felt so sorry for him. My own mind was such a jumble of thoughts and feelings, I didn't see how he would be able to think clearly.

I spent some time in Jill's room that morning, looking for a new piece to fit the puzzle. What I found only increased my anxiety. From a letter, I learned that Eddie had stopped in Evansville on his way to Florida. I assumed that's where they were headed and wondered how far they might have traveled by now.

I realized I should probably call Eddie's parents. I had no idea if the police would pick him up, too, or just Jill. We had a Lebanon phone directory, but when I dialed the number I learned it was now unlisted. Of course, the operator would not give it to me, but she did connect me with her supervisor, who connected me with her supervisor who connected me with another supervisor. After telling the story many times, I was finally connected to Eddie's home. I hated to tell his mother; she had heartache enough without me adding to it. But I didn't want her to be surprised by the police either.

Then I began to remember commitments Jill had left behind. It was Saturday. Tomorrow she would be expected to play the organ at the little Baptist church up the street. They would need to know now, in order to get a substitute. At first I didn't know who to call or what to tell them. Then I thought of Ann, a lovely, quiet person who was active in the church. Without ever intending to, I began to tell her the whole story. That day Ann affirmed a part of Jill that had been hidden from me. She had seen only the pretty, well-mannered, outgoing girl who played the organ and piano and led the children's choir. She was as surprised to hear about the Jill I knew, as I was to be reminded of the one I had known long ago. I needed that. In the days to come that picture of Jill helped me reconstruct our relationship.

THE END OF THE ROAD
AND THE WAY OUT

10

JUST AS PAINTING can be therapeutic, writing this book has helped Jill and me. We have shared as never before, we have cried, and we have grown—talking about subjects that we never had, without resentment or anger. Especially revealing was her version of that night in August. For years, I thought the worst: that she spent the night in a motel with Eddie. But that was not how it was. . . .

"Eddie and I had talked about my leaving home. Always, there were two parts of me—one said to leave, get out. The other said: stay, you don't really want to run away. Even as I sat writing a letter to say I was leaving, that other part of me was scared and lonely and didn't want to go.

"As I crawled out my bedroom window, the frame slid back down on me with a thud. I was crying from the pain as I ran up into the court.

"Eddie was waiting in his car. I didn't think he would still be around. I told him to get out of here. Then I sat down, hidden behind some bushes in the neighbor's yard. I could hear dad calling me. I wanted to answer him, to go back to my own room.

"But, instead, I ran and ran—through the woods and up the hill to Newburgh Road and the high school. I stopped at a Red Bird station and called Eddie; he wasn't back at the motel yet. The guy in the station made some wisecracks about me getting dumped. I ran out of there and onto the state hospital grounds, past the armory, and into a little wooded area. I needed to stop and rest; I felt like I couldn't get enough air, and I couldn't stop crying.

"Then some guy and a girl came. I left, running past the stadium and over a fence onto the golf course in Wesselman Park. I tore my jeans on the fence. My bare feet were bruised and sore, and my throat and eyes ached. Anyone who saw me must have thought I was crazy—running wildly and crying all the time. I crawled into a corner of a shelter house in the park. It was a hot August night, but I was cold—cold and crying and shaking all over.

"I don't know why I ran away, except that there was a pressure inside me all the time, and sometimes it grew and grew. Then I had to run. I don't know what I was running to. I just felt driven to run, away from everything and everybody—to run and run until I was exhausted.

"I knew who my parents wanted me to be. I just didn't know who I was, who I wanted to be. I felt so not-okay, and I was sure my parents felt the same way about me.

"Very early the next morning I went to the Greer

Motel. Eddie told me his mother had called to say the police were looking for me, and he had better cut out. He was going to take me home as soon as he showered and dressed. I was only there about ten minutes when the police came after me. I was glad.

"Once I was in the backseat of the squad car, I began to notice there were no handles on the doors, no way to open them from the inside or to roll a window down. There was a glass divider that separated me from the policemen in front. They were laughing as they radioed in, 'We've picked up your wild runaway.' Their voices mocked me."

" 'Cigarette?' they asked, holding the pack out to me. 'Why'd you run away?' "

"To both questions, I just shook my head. All at once, I realized they weren't taking me home."

" 'Where are we going? Where are you taking me?' "

"I was frightened when they said the police station. I wondered if they were going to put me in a cell. Then, the car pulled into a closed-in area like a garage. There was a security guard at the door. When another door was unlocked, we entered a large room that looked like a big office. Typewriters were clicking, phones ringing, and I could hear the police radio in the background. I sat on a bench looking at the floor. I remember thinking that the light-colored tile was like the floors at school.

"There was another girl sitting with me. I began to wonder what she had done. She looked 'skuzzy.' Did I look like that to all these people? Someone told me I would have to wait here until my folks came. That really scared me. I wasn't afraid of anything they might do; I was afraid to face them. I hadn't wanted to cause them this kind of trouble. It seemed like I sat there a long time, staring at the floor and listening to the sounds around me. They took the other girl off some place, and I was alone.

"Then the door opened, and my mom and dad were there. I didn't know what to say or do. Mom came over and put her hand on me. I don't remember much of what happened after that, except that the officer was blaming my parents and it made me feel terrible. . . ."

I no longer recall all the details of that interview with Captain Kleeman. But Jill was right, he blamed us. When he discovered Gene was a Baptist minister, it seemed to solve the problem for him: an overly strict Baptist home, a child in natural rebellion. Period. He explained that Jill now had a record that would be on file until she was eighteen, but that juvenile records were private. *What's the difference?* I thought. *You know. All these people know. The whole world knows we're crummy parents.*

He told us there were two alternatives: either agree to counseling or follow the court procedure. Naturally, we opted for counseling, and Jill agreed.

Once we were away from that place, the fear was gone, and the guilt returned. Hadn't he as much as said it was our fault? There was anger, too. Weren't we supposed to make our child mind? Weren't we supposed to know where she was going, what she was doing, and when she'd be home? Were you to let teenagers do as they pleased? And how did you live under those rules? If you reported your child as a runaway, the child got a record. Either court action or counseling must follow. If you didn't, you could be charged with negligence and being unfit. I felt we had been dropped through a trapdoor into some kind of prison.

But Jill had run away when I was job hunting, and this type of distraction was just what I needed. I had begun to look for a job early in the spring; if I went back to work for awhile, it might be a tonic for my ego. My self-esteem had been badly bent. For one thing, Gene's job was different here. This was no small-town church where the pastor's wife served as a Jill of all trades. The truth was, I just didn't fit into his work anymore.

Yoke that to the sense of failure and guilt I felt over Jill, and you had a person whose self-image was dragging in the dust. I also knew it was imperative to my emotional health that Jill go away to college, which would require additional income.

The first employment tests I took were poison. I couldn't see what they had to do with bookkeeping: "If A and B are equal to C, and D equals half as much as A, what is the sum?" That company never even sent me a rejection letter.

Then Gene brought home *Guidelines,* a paper published by the local council of churches, advertising their need for a part-time bookkeeper. He convinced me to call for an interview. But Jill ran away before I could keep this appointment.

Because we knew the administrator of the council, Gene felt free to explain why I hadn't been there and set up another appointment. With this interview pending, I was forced to remain composed, despite what was going on inside me. I kept the appointment and was hired.

That job was the best thing that could have happened to me. For two days a week, I had to think about something besides our problems with Jill. I couldn't worry about her, I had no time to belittle myself, and I couldn't rehash the counseling sessions. I was a good bookkeeper, and the recognition I received made me feel competent again.

AN ENDING
AND A BEGINNING

11

OUR MANDATORY COUNSELING SESSIONS brought further turmoil. Jill returned from an initial session that included inkblot tests and proclaimed, "They think I'm crazy. I'm not going back."

We assured her the tests were to discover how smart she was, not how dumb. The counseling would be more effective if the counselor understood her completely, including her intellectual and psychological development.

My reaction to our first session was that I had been judged guilty without a hearing. The counselor seemed to have made some assumptions about Gene and me before she ever saw us. Gene was a Baptist clergyman; therefore we were straitlaced, narrow-minded, and forced our religious beliefs on our children. Gene spent too much time with his work and not enough at home. Behind every question lay these preconceived theories, and some others not as clearly defined. If I prefaced a response with "I guess"—a term I used frequently—I was pounced on.

"Do you 'guess,' Mrs. Ton?"—as if she never listened to what I was saying, only the manner in which I said it. When I made a statement, she repeated it, telling me what she heard me saying—a current approach to listening. But if I hadn't meant what she thought, I was unable to change her misconception.

I never once felt "heard." My guilt feelings grew with each session. If I was truly responsible for the agony Jill was experiencing—if I had warped her life in some way—then I might also hurt my other children.

I needed someone to understand *me*, to know the extent of my pain. Both Gene and I needed someone to recognize that we were two parents hurting for our child and for ourselves—afraid and humiliated. We needed recognition of the good things we had done, and acceptance, in spite of our mistakes. Instead we found more blame. It seemed a predrawn conclusion that we, and we alone, were responsible for what our child was becoming. At this counseling center, the child was the victim, the parents the villain.

I went as long as I dared. Then I told Gene, "I'm never going back. I can't. Please understand. I can't."

Something awful was happening inside me. Something I can only explain in the words I whispered to Gene late one night: "I feel there is almost no more of me left. What will happen when I'm all gone?"

Even when he held me close, this fear wouldn't go away. Only now it was a fear for myself. I had allowed Jill's problems to consume me. They were not her problems anymore. They were mine. Too often, I lay in bed and thought how easy it would be to close the garage doors, turn on the car engine, and go to sleep. The blackness of death seemed too inviting.

But some place inside me a warning signal sounded. I didn't really want to curl up in the fetal position and accept blankness. I wanted to fight for life. The life preservers were already there—floating around, just waiting for me to grab them. My mind returned to the insight I had received when Jeff shared his experience at camp: Jeff was not my own. He was *God's* child. A person complete without me. Neither was Jill my own. Jill was *God's* child, too. Gene and I had only been the medium that gave her life. And this life had been begun with love and the conscious desire to have another child. The miracle that took place in my womb following that initial act was God's. We had no more control over it than we did the labor contractions that forced her to the moment of birth.

God had created the person she was. I had not given her talents, God had. My accomplishment on the piano consisted of the scale and chopsticks. Jill not only played the piano, she felt it. She alone had exercised this gift and developed her potential. Her scholastic ability, her sensitivity to persons with special needs—all these were part of her uniqueness. I could claim no credit for them. But neither could I take the blame, if she was now making some poor choices.

With this new awareness, the heaviness and the hurt and the guilt began to diminish. Now I could look at Jill in a new way. She had been given into my care, and I had done my best. Surely when God gave me that responsibility, he knew I would make mistakes. But he trusted me in spite of that. Now I could begin to return that trust. I could pray again, without prefacing everything with why? And I could release her to his care. Finally I could say, "Lord, here is the child you gave me. I have given her love and care. Forgive me for the mistakes I have made. I return this child to you almost grown. I trust you with her, because you have allowed me to see your presence in another child I love. Thank you for them, Lord."

Then on January 18, 1973, I chose to read *The Prophet* by Kahlil Gibran to commemorate my father's death the year before. A friend had given this book to me then, and I began with the selection on death. Then I noticed one "On Children."

And a woman who held a babe against her bosom said, Speak to us of Children.

And he said:
Your children are not your children.
They are the sons and daughters of Life's longing for itself.
They come through you but not from you,
And though they are with you yet they belong not to you.

You may give them your love but not your thoughts,
For they have their own thoughts.
You may house their bodies but not their souls,
For their souls dwell in the house of tomorrow, which you cannot visit, not even in your dreams.
You may strive to be like them, but seek not to make them like you.
For life goes not backward nor tarries with yesterday.
You are the bows from which your children as living arrows are sent forth.

The archer sees the mark upon the path of the infinite,
and He bends you with His might that His arrows may go
swift and far.
Let your bending in the archer's hand be for gladness;
For even as He loves the arrow that flies, so He loves the
bow that is stable.

"Your children are not your children"—how affirming
this was to my growing conviction! They belonged to
themselves and God. I sat there awestruck. All the time I
had been angry and full of hate toward God, he had
already moved ahead of me and put resources at my
disposal, to be used when I was ready.

I felt like the jury had returned, and the verdict was
clearly not guilty. I wanted to shout, *"I am not guilty!"*

Then I relaxed, much as I do when I shower after a day
of mowing our huge lawn. I lift my face up into the water,
and as the dirt runs down the drain, the tiredness goes
with it. That day, the guilt, the failure, and the fear
washed away. I felt revived and refreshed: a new person.

Now instead of dwelling on what I had or hadn't done,
I could think about myself and the person I wanted to be.
I realized that I had to change! I was the only person I
could change anyway. I must learn to love Jill as God
loved her, which was exactly as she was right now. "But it
will be so hard," I said.

"I know," He answered.

Gene and I began to talk again. We began to search for
some common directions. He had been too soft; I, too
hard. Maybe we could melt together into a moderate
consistency.

One of the first steps was to show Jill her relationship
to God was private. Of course, it always had been. Now

we could act on that belief, trusting God to work independently in her life. There would be no more prodding Jill to our moral standards, no more pushing church. I felt I should be the one to tell her this; I needed to lay the base for a new relationship. It would be a long time before Jill went into a church again.

RUN AWAY, LITTLE GIRL

12

IT WAS AN ORDINARY Sunday morning. I sat in my usual place near the front, only half listening. The hymns we sang were songs of praise and thanksgiving. As I mouthed the words, I silently prayed, "Forgive me, you know I'm singing a lie." Soon the congregation settled back for the sermon, and some listened. I did. It was a discipline I had acquired in seventeen years as a pastor's wife, and now I needed to listen.

What was it he just read? Something teased my mind and was gone. Now what was it? The Scripture was the story of the prodigal son. I had heard it hundreds of times. So what had suddenly struck me? Yes, the father *let* the son leave home. He simply let him go.

How could he do that? He probably guessed what was going to happen. Or maybe that's the most important point of all; maybe he didn't know what might happen or if he would ever see his son again. And still, he let him go.

All my life, I had understood this parable as an analogy of how God works with individuals. I always knew it was a story of free will and sin, repentance and forgiveness. But I had never thought of it as a story of freedom: a son's freedom to leave home, and the father's freedom to let go. I wondered. Could I be that kind of parent? Could I be free enough to let Jill go?

My mind searched the story for similarities and meanings. Jill had her "share of the inheritance." As a child, she had been cherished and cared for. She had been taught about God, had expressed her own belief, and been baptized. She had been provided with all the materials to grow physically and mentally. Her inheritance was rich.

Gene and I talked about this idea. Did we trust the wealth of that inheritance? Did we really believe God would continue to work in her life if we let go? Was it a responsible thing to do? Obviously God extended freedom to many people who appeared incapable of handling it. Could we let Jill go?

On the other hand, could we force her to stay? Not unless we made her a prisoner. In March, she would be eighteen, legally free. In June, we hoped she would graduate from high school. Time was running out.

It was not an easy decision. She might take off the day we told her; a part of us expected just that. Looking back now, this was the most important decision we ever made; we decided to let her run away.

The hardest thing I have ever done was to walk into her room and say, "Okay, little girl, run away." I always approached her door hestitantly, anyway; a knock usually brought an impatient, haughty "What?" I would walk away without even answering, thinking "So, go jump in the lake!"

That night my knock brought the anticipated response. Still, I opened the door and went in.

Her room always seemed too full: twin beds, a desk and chair that almost touched her long dresser, and two bookshelves crammed with miscellanea rose above discarded clothes, crumpled papers, dirty dishes, and various other collections. Now, in late January, a mound of wrinkled blankets lay in the center of her bed, exactly where she had crawled out of them that morning and, most likely, where she had crawled in the night before.

"Shut the door. I'm trying to see," she began.

I replied by slamming the door hard.

Jill was sitting cross-legged on the end of her bed rolling her hair up in enormous rollers. I really had disturbed her, because the mirror was on the back of the door I had just opened.

I sat down on the edge of the other bed and watched her continue to set her hair. Jill snapped her tongue against her teeth and squirmed impatiently. It was part of the game we played. Usually, I would have responded, "What's the matter, do you have something stuck in your teeth?" I let it pass this time around.

"Dad and I have talked," I began, "and we agree you can leave if you want to. If going back to Lebanon is what you want, we won't stop you."

She paused in rolling one curler, and her expression changed for an instant. Then, as though I had caused her to roll it wrong, she took the curler out and began again.

"The decision is up to you, Jill. Like you've been telling us, it's your life. If you mess it up, it will be your responsibility, too."

Jill set the rollers aside and began to brush the back of her hair idly. I waited for some response, and then began again.

107

"We love you, Jill. That may be hard to believe, but we do. We'd like you to stay. But if you really want to go, then leave like an adult. Pack your belongings, tell us good-bye, and walk out the front door."

Jill listened, silent and immobile. She wore the same mask we had come to know so well: chin firmly set, eyes speaking messages I couldn't understand. For a brief second, I thought she was going to reply. But the flicker of animation faded back into a sullen stare.

I cried as I lay in bed that night. But the tears indicated the release of tension, rather than its presence. I remember thinking, *Don't cry, you'll get your hair all wet, and you have to go to work in the morning.* I smiled. It had been a long time since I had smiled in the blackness of our room.

A CRACK IN THE WALL

13

JILL BEGAN to save her earnings for a trip to Lebanon. When she had enough for her airplane ticket, she told us she would go the following weekend. We asked how she planned to get to the airport.

"I thought you said I could make all my own decisions," she replied.

"You may go, but we don't want you to. And we won't help," I added. We didn't need to. Jill managed all the details herself.

By the time Friday came, Gene and I were really worried. Jill came home after school to get her suitcases. A car was parked out front. She simply said, "I'm leaving now."

"I see you are," I replied haughtily.

"I don't know what you're so spastic about, you said I could do whatever I want."

I tried to explain she was free to go, but she did not have our permission. Jill couldn't see the difference.

All weekend, we tried to keep our minds from imagining what she was doing or wondering if she would come home at all. By the time we returned from Sunday morning service, Jill was back.

After lunch, she remained at the table instead of rushing to her room. She was still there when I began loading the dishwasher. Wondering what was coming next, I gripped the dishes firmly to keep from dropping them. I sensed she wanted to say something, and I wasn't sure I wanted to hear. But something urged me to speak, even though words often formed in my mind now that never came out.

Finally I asked, "How was the trip?" I had planned to sound casual, but my voice reflected my nervousness.

"Okay." She paused so long I thought that was all. Then as I moved toward the door, she added, "Nobody was at the airport to pick me up."

For a second, I thought *Well, that's your friends for you. I told you not to go.* Instead I just said, "Oh?" and edged onto a chair beside her. Ordinarily, she would have gotten up and walked away. But this time, she didn't. Her words found a hairline crack in our wall. Haltingly, cautiously—interspersed with deep breaths—she began to talk.

Word followed word, each one eroding a little more, widening the crack. I responded in monosyllables, scarcely daring to breathe. I had no idea what had turned her on, or what might cause her to stop.

She had waited over an hour at the Indianapolis airport before Eddie finally picked her up. He had forgotten the time. They went to a Lebanon High basketball game. Some of her old friends hardly spoke to her; she felt they went out of their way to avoid her. A policeman

112

friend of hers said very little, but seemed to watch her every move. After the game, Eddie took her to a party at a farmhouse nearby. As soon as she walked in, she knew this was no ordinary party. Kids were lying around the room. There was no laughing and little or no talking. She went into the kitchen with Eddie, and then she knew. Kids out there were getting ready to shoot up. Jill was frightened and asked to leave. She was angry that he had brought her to something like that. They argued, but he finally took her back to Lebanon. She began to realize that Eddie had forgotten dates and times and incidents. The changes that had been evident to us broke through her consciousness. For the first time, she saw what was happening to him. She had even watched Eddie and Mike fight so violently that Eddie had to be hospitalized. Never before had she seen two people threaten each other with a gun as they had.

Once started, she couldn't stop. She talked on, telling me every detail. What she said; what Eddie said. Everything around us seemed to disappear, as though we were suspended in that moment of time. Then she cried as she admitted that Eddie was a drug addict and might never change. The whole house was still. Gene and the boys knew not to disrupt that conversation. This child, who had shut herself off for 2½ years, talked the entire afternoon.

The trip we had dreaded—would have done anything to prevent—turned out to be the best thing that could have happened, for Jill found herself careening around a bend in her road. There would be many more, but she was on her way home.

Driving to church early that evening, I shared all that

113

had taken place with Gene. And, in my own mind, I pondered a mystery. What had made me keep still? What silenced all the I-told-you-so's? I didn't know, and I still don't. I listened, and for the first time, I heard her pain. Not my own, but hers! I saw a girl who felt deeply for a boy who was ruining his life, a person who had seen something very wrong and recognized it, a child who needed to tell her mother how frightened she was. It was a part of Jill I thought had vanished. Now that I had let go, I was able to see her in a new way. And she was free from the stranglehold of my guilt, free to come out of that ugly brown cocoon she had spun around herself for protection. I began to assure myself that the Jill of the past months was not the whole person. I determined to affirm that, not only to myself, but to her. Even though Jill was still withdrawn, I now believed in resurrection.

That affirmation was soon to be tested. Gene and I had done a great deal of thinking about the times Jill had run away. We became convinced she had been playing a game of hide-and-seek. Jill was an intelligent girl. If she had wanted to get lost, she could have done so. But she wanted to be found and brought home. We realized this was not the solution; she had to come home by herself. And she couldn't do that unless we stopped playing "It."

One night when Jill came into our bedroom to tell us she was leaving, we did just that. We repeated all that we had told her before and added that we wouldn't chase after her. "You're responsible for yourself, Jill."

Her face flushed, and her eyes went wild. She could not stand still. "I can't help it. I have to go. It's building up in me again." She pressed her hands over her face as she left the room.

114

For a long time, we could hear her moving around in her room. Then the house was still. Were we really sure we were doing the right thing? No, but we were free, and we went to sleep.

In the morning, I listened outside Jill's door. I didn't hear a sound. Very cautiously, I opened it a crack. In the middle of her bed was a heap of blankets. And under them, Jill was sound asleep.

There would be other nights, like summer reruns on TV. For days we would watch Jill become more and more nervous, increasingly irritable and defiant. Then she would come and say she was leaving. We would go through our part, assuring her of our love but telling her she had to decide for herself. The old game was over. Perhaps a new one had begun, but Jill never ran away from home again.

LIKE THE
GENTLE TOUCH OF SPRING

14

EVANSVILLE IS BEAUTIFUL in the spring. The drive down Bellemeade from our home to the church is full of surprises. Magnolias, pink and white dogwoods, red buds, azaleas—all take their turn bursting into bloom. This spring was particularly lovely. I was beginning to breathe deeper, to relax a little: to experience new life.

Jill had her eighteenth birthday in March, and she was still at home. She had filled out scholarship applications and admission forms for college. The talk of returning to Lebanon had all but stopped. Now she just dreamed of going back to see "her" class graduate. It looked like we were on our way.

In April, I experienced one of God's mini-miracles. We had lived in Evansville over 2½ years. During all that time, we were hurting badly. But we had confided in no one. Only once had I reached out for help. On the Sunday morning after Jill ran away, I asked one of the older ladies in our congregation to pray for Gene. I explained very quickly that we were having some problems with Jill, and Gene was upset that morning. Upset?

We both felt defeated. I could hardly make myself go to church that day. Gene had two sermons to preach.

Gene had also tried to share our anguish once. In a Wednesday evening group, he had dared to admit that ministers sometimes have problems they can't handle. To which a man in the group responded, "I don't want to hear about it. I don't like to think ministers have problems—it destroys my image." Needless to say, Gene backed off.

So because of our pride and other people's images, we had struggled alone. From time to time, I would hear of a family experiencing some of the same problems, but I never thought sharing our situation might help.

Then one day I learned the youngest daughter of some good friends had converted to Mormonism. Now all three of their children had chosen that direction. Our expression of faith was important to Charlie and Roberta, so I knew how they must be hurting. I knew they were troubled by the same age-old questions: What did we do wrong? Why did God let this happen?

I wanted to help. But how could I, when I couldn't help myself? I could at least tell them I understood. But only if I were willing to let them know about Jill. I wasn't sure I was ready to make myself that vulnerable.

Then I received a letter asking me to contribute to a book of Lenten meditations for our church. The short writings were to speak about resurrection. Realizing that my children were not my own—that I was not completely responsible for them—had brought new life to me. I saw this as an opportunity to share a resurrection experience with members of our church, particularly Charlie and Roberta. And I could do it anonymously by making my meditation a letter to "Dear Friends" and signing it "Another Parent."

But my meditation never appeared in that booklet. Before it could be printed, I called our assistant pastor and told him to hold it. I wasn't ready to expose myself even that much.

The nagging thought, however, kept recurring, urging me to share what had happened. I made all kinds of excuses: It would be like telling on Jill. What do Charlie and Roberta care how I feel? They'll think I'm butting in.

Finally on April 18, 1973, I wrote them directly, enclosing a copy of the meditation letter I had written and the reading "On Children."

I wrote that letter to help someone else. Instead, it was me who found healing. At last I had dared to expose my hurt, and someone moved to help by applying love and acceptance. Why had I waited so long?

Only a few weeks ago when I told Roberta about this book, she asked if I wanted to use the letters.

"I still have them," she explained. "I get them out and read them sometimes."

When I saw those letters again, I had some strange feelings. I'm not sure how to tag them—wonder, maybe. God had used my letters, was still using them. From somewhere deep inside me came a soft, tremulous "Wow!"

It was that kind of spring. A time to walk a little bit slower, to speak a little softer—a gentle time. As April turned into May, this feeling persisted.

Even Jill's trip to Lebanon for graduation seemed less threatening. This time her older brother Jack took her. Knowing he was along helped.

Jill came home excited at sharing Eddie's graduation with his family. Besides the formal activities, she had spent an evening in their home, joining in the fun by playing the piano. She appreciated their warm acceptance of her and enjoyed the evening even more, I think, because she had closed herself off from this kind of sharing with us. Jill never mentioned drugs, and I didn't question her. Sometime later we heard Eddie had been busted. I tried to express my concern for him, but Jill didn't respond.

Now our goal was becoming a reality: Jill would graduate. So much depended on that diploma; it was her passport to the future, whether or not she chose to attend college. I felt like we were graduating, too—from a certain parental responsibility.

Jill had already asked if Eddie could come for graduation. Again we threw the decision back to her.

"But can he come here to the house and go with you?" she replied. We reminded her we had never said Eddie couldn't come to our house or stopped her from seeing him. If Eddie's going with us would make her day special, fine.

So Eddie went to Roberts Stadium with us. He was still handsome, but now he reminded me of Jill when she walked in her sleep—eyes wide open but not really present. It was spooky and heartbreaking.

Every mother reminisces as she watches her child process to "Pomp and Circumstance": the day the doctor gave the confirming yes, the first stirrings of life, the first day of school, piano recitals, baptism, school programs, and proms. It was like that when Jack graduated—a certain feeling of fulfillment, of its being okay that he was now a young man. But with Jill, I felt a desire to go back and grab hold of all the time wasted to collect all the broken pieces and try to put them together. I cried at Jack's graduation, I cried at Jeff's, and I'm certain to cry at Joe's. At Jill's, I wept.

At the house afterwards, Jill opened her gift, and she and Eddie ate some ice cream and cake. Then they were off to the parties. It was over. The day we had yearned for had come and gone. There was no triumph.

SO HIGH
YOU CAN'T GET OVER IT

15

ALL THIS TIME, Gene had maintained some relationship with Jill. He would extend his trust again and again, only to have it stepped on. But he was able to handle each situation as it arose and then let go. Because he didn't store any resentment, Jill turned to him more and more. She had learned that her dad often replied yes, while my answer was usually no. I felt privileges should be earned; he didn't see it that way. I became angry and jealous of the slightest rapport between them, even though I knew one of us had to stay in touch with her. I felt that if Gene had to bear all her frustrations—if he had to stay with her all day—he would understand what it was like.

Each day I would determine to be different, to react more calmly. But Jill seemed equally determined to bait me, thwarting my best resolves. One day followed another, the same as before. I wanted to love Jill openly, but we were unable to establish a new relationship.

I became anxious for her to leave for college. She had received a scholarship from the state scholarship commission for her tuition at Indiana University in

Bloomington. Soon she would attend freshman orienta-
tion, a two-day visit to acquaint new students and their
parents with the campus. I said I had to work; Gene
could take her.

I really wanted to go—to be part of this experience—
but I wouldn't admit it. I wanted Jill to ask me, expecting
her to be more mature than I was. When Gene questioned me, I replied, "You go ahead. You two will get
along fine. She doesn't want me to go."

Jill and her father came home from IU full of excitement and anticipation for the fall. I had shut myself out
and felt lonely.

The remaining days were spent collecting things for
college: sheets, blankets, towels, soap. All the personal
articles of a home had to be assembled just for her. As she
packed, Jill cleaned her room. Bag after bag was carried
out to the trash full of fragments of her life: old school
papers, books, pictures, bits of ribbon and dried flowers,
posters, and bundles of letters.

"Mother, what do you want me to do with my flute . . .
my Barbie dolls?" There was a finality to the process, as
though she would never be a part of that room again.

Then there was just tonight. Tomorrow Gene would
take her to Bloomington. Again I had said I had to work.
But I still hoped Jill would give some indication she
wanted me. She never did; she couldn't, I suppose, anymore than I could say I wanted to go along. Two obsti-
nate women separated by a wall they had built themselves.

At breakfast that morning, I wanted to reach out, to
say, "I'm going to call and tell Fran I'm going with you,"
or "Be a good girl," or to ask, "Have you got everything?"

Instead I talked to Gene and the boys as if Jill weren't leaving. When I left for work, I said good-bye as casually as if I'd see her at supper.

Then, I sat stiffly at my desk, staring at books that didn't seem to make sense. There was still time. I could call home; I could still say something to her. The phone rang.

"Good morning, Evansville Area Council of Churches."

"Mom?"

I scarcely recognized Jill's voice.

"Dad told me to call and say good-bye."

Melt! I screamed at myself, *melt!* "Okay. You're leaving now?"

"Yes."

"Well, good-bye then."

"Bye."

I put the phone down slowly, hoping to hear Jill's voice again. I left the office, went down the hall to the rest room, and let the tears run down my cheeks.

The next morning, after everyone was gone, I went into Jill's bedroom. Working too fast, I stripped the beds, mattress pads and all. As I returned from the laundry room, I picked up the vacuum and cleaned the floor. Never had I worked so hard. I scrubbed the walls and washed and waxed the hardwood floor. I vacuumed the empty dresser drawers and the closet. Then I rearranged the furniture and made the beds. By supper, the room was antiseptically clean. It looked so nice—just the way I had planned when I painted the furniture and made the drapes and bedspreads. The door I had wanted to open for such a long time now stood open. Every time I walked down the hall I looked into this sunshiny room, but only the pink eyes of a furry white bunny stared back at me.

One week and then two passed with little word from Jill. People asked if I missed her. I knew I was expected to answer yes. But I only felt relieved. Jill was where she wanted to be: away from home. I had been lonely for her when we had lived in the same house. Now those feelings were natural and seemed more comfortable.

Slowly, her letters began to come. Jill had always been an avid letter writer. Now the letters came to us—long letters, filled with news about her classes and professors, the people she was meeting, and her roommate, Karen. She shared more of herself than she had for years. And I wrote back, filling my letters with bits and pieces of our daily lives that she had cut herself off from.

I thought back to the note writing we had done. Jill wrote long, rambling notes, expressing her anger and pent-up emotions. For a long time, I replied, trying to express some of my feelings. Then I withheld even that part of me. Now I realized that had been our only honest communication; I never should have stopped it. As I read each letter, I recognized how much we had lost. But I still didn't know how to break through the wall between us. Letters, like paper airplanes, could be sent sailing over the top, but were ineffective as chisels.

Then Jill began to call home. I really didn't know why; she just wanted to talk. Gene and I began to joke about how she had said nothing for three years and now that it cost money, she wanted to talk. We might have reminded her, "You can write it for ten cents!" Instead, we encouraged her. Something was happening. But we could hardly believe what we suspected.

130

Then one day Jill began to cry during one of her calls. "I think I'm homesick," she stammered.

As soon as she hung up, I called Gene at the office. "Guess what? Jill's homesick!" I laughed as the tears ran down my cheeks. Jill loved us; she valued her home and her family. Finally she had stuck the tip of her nose out of that cocoon and was blinking in the light.

We had let Jill go because of my interpretation of the parable of the prodigal son. And now, she was on her way back. Could I run to meet her? What if I ran headlong into that solid brick wall? A part of me still wanted to make her come to me, to make her—crawl?

A CHISEL FOR THE WALLS

16

THE HAUNTING STRAINS of "Greensleeves" flowed
through the church on this Christmas Eve, 1973. For a
moment I relaxed and absorbed its rich melody, filling
me with sadness and hope. I thought about Jill as I often
did. Was my daughter really so different from me? She
was a strange mixture, a paradox—an angry rebel and a
homesick little girl. But wasn't I two people also? An
uptight woman—feeling unneeded, unwanted, so much
a failure—carrying a lot of anger, hurt, and jealousy. But
at the same time, a wife and mother—a woman who loved
her husband, enjoyed her kids, and found fulfillment in
being a mother—sometimes capable of being quite sensitive and understanding. I knew which person I wanted to
be, but more often than not I found myself reacting as
the other.

It had been nine months since I had recognized the
need for change in my own life. But that change was
imperceptible; it was as if I had been jogging in place,

using up a lot of energy, getting nowhere.

Then Gene gave me a copy of Thomas Harris's *I'm OK, You're OK* for Christmas. It was not easy reading for me, but there were snatches I could grab hold of. I found myself thinking, *Yeah! I see what he means. That's how it is.* I kept returning to these new ideas, getting the book out again to read parts over. The more I read, the clearer I could see myself, as though a door had been opened that cleared the condensation from my mirror.

One night I noticed that Lockyear Business College was going to offer a course using Harris's book as the main text. I mentioned it to Gene, who immediately urged me to register. The more he promoted the idea, the more excuses I made: "I'm working, there isn't time." "I'm not smart enough." On I went, with Gene pointing out the fallacy in every excuse. Looking back, I realize he was as anxious about me as both of us were about Jill. He wanted his wife back, as well as his daughter.

With Gene waiting outside the door like an anxious parent, I went into the admissions office and signed up for my only college course. Those two class hours became an important part of my week. Sometimes I became excited, as I saw the possibility of integrating the ideas into my own life. Sometimes frightened, as long-held thought patterns, behavior modes, and prejudices were challenged. Yet I was always stimulated to go a little deeper and learn more.

How can I explain what happened to me? I don't know. Much of what I heard was not entirely new, only presented in a new way. Much of it was common sense that others may have assimilated naturally. I only know that in the spring of 1974 something life-changing happened to me. I was stretched in such a way that I never returned to my original shape.

As a person, I had ranked myself not-okay. I had a rebel daughter. My husband had a string of letters after his name; I was just a high-school graduate. I had no special talents or gifts to speak of.

But now I began to see that the volume could be turned down on that recording. I came to recognize the different and sometimes conflicting parts of my personality. I was not alone. Even Paul had experienced this same struggle in Romans 7: "I don't understand myself at all, for I really want to do what is right, but I can't. I do what I don't want to—what I hate. . . . No matter which way I turn I can't make myself do right."

Then I learned how to analyze my relationships with other persons: to track down the feelings these relationships evoked and move toward understanding. I was learning how to become the person I wanted to be—a new person. Those words had a familiar ring. Wasn't this the essence of the good news of Jesus Christ? I was an okay person, loved by God, a child of God, and I could become a new person. I had listened to that broadcast for a long time; but announced to me now in a new form, I heard it.

In that class I found a tool for understanding myself and other people—even Jill! Here was a microscope under which my ways of reacting could be viewed and dissected.

The first time I used this method, it happened almost without conscious effort. Jack was waiting to get his income tax refund, a sizable amount. All he could talk about was how he was going to spend it. He promoted first one hair-brained idea and then another.

He ought to pay some of his bills, I thought, *or, at the very least, he should save it in case something goes wrong with his car.* Without realizing it, I found myself analyzing my reaction. What made me so angry? Where did my own feelings come from? My parents were pretty close with money; they had to be. But when money came unexpectedly, they did something fun with it. Bam! It struck home. I went into the bedroom to talk to Gene.

"Honey, when we get some extra money, a windfall, what do we do with it?"

He only thought a minute before replying, "We usually spend it on something extra, something we ordinarily couldn't get."

"Right!" I broke in. "And what did we do several years back when our income was really limited?"

"Well, the same thing, I guess."

"Yes!" I exploded, "and sometimes we just blew it. That's what my parents used to do, and that's what we do. No wonder that's what Jack dreams of doing!"

I wasn't mad at Jack anymore. I understood how he was feeling and could apologize for getting so upset.

That's a simple occurrence, but it was the first time I had worked through the trackdown process and saw that it worked. Now if I could begin that same process with Jill, maybe I could get the same results.

It wasn't very long until I had a chance to try. Jill wanted to join the annual spring migration of college students to Florida. She wrote to ask what we thought. That in itself was an indication that our relationship was changing.

When I read her letter, all kinds of feelings were

triggered. The strongest was anger. *Okay,* I thought, *what are the different voices saying?* Part of me had a great deal to say: *Why should she go to Florida while I'm working to help pay her college bills? Besides, I know what goes on in Florida during spring break; I've heard all about it.*

But didn't I hear something else? From somewhere deep inside, a little voice I seldom listened to was saying, *It does sound like fun!*

I took time to sort through all my feelings and began to think, *If she could get a part-time job to earn the money or to replace it . . .*

When I got around to responding to Jill's letter, I told it just like that. Then I closed by saying, "Make your own decision. It won't be easy. Few decisions are all right or all wrong. Most of them are good, better, or best, and those are the toughies. What you really want to know is, will we be mad? No! We won't."

Kerplunk! One brick fell to the ground.

Jill responded by calling and announcing, after some preliminary conversation, "I've decided not to go to Florida after all. You know, it just isn't easy to make all your own decisions. It isn't even fun." This was an important insight for a strong-willed young girl who had often shouted, "It's my life. Just let me alone."

There would be other incidents, some far more complex, cutting deeply into our value system. During one of these times, I was trying to categorize my thoughts to know how to relate to Jill. She was already hurting deeply from the mistake she had made. Jeff came downstairs and sat on the steps saying, "What's up, moms?"

I told him what had happened. And then I said, "Right now I would just like to hold Jill again and make everything all right for her, like I could by kissing your bumped knees."

Jeff just sort of nodded, his eyes filling with tears, and went back upstairs. Later that day I found this poem lying on my bed with a note that said "For Mom."

Come my little child,
Let me hold you in my arms.
I will chase all the bad things away.
Oh, but little child,
You are too big for my arms.
The day I could help you was yesterday.

Oh, my little baby,
I tried to help, but you couldn't see.
Now I can only watch while you sit and cry.
Oh, my big grown girl,
Fortify yourself and hold to faith.
Patience and understanding will open the door.

Come my little child,
Let me hold you in my arms.
I will chase all the bad things away.
Oh, but little child,
You are too big for my arms.
The day I could help you was yesterday.

Once I wouldn't have shared my feelings with Jeff in that way. His poem would never have been written, and I wouldn't have known the support of his love and understanding.

The tool worked, not only with Jill, but now with the

boys and Gene. I had found a lever to open my daily life to the Christian values I knew, and I went to work. Without realizing the impact of what she was saying, Jill later told her grandmother, "My mother has really changed." When grandma shared this with me, I felt okay. The new me was showing! And I was beginning to think Jill was okay, too!

COME TO THE PARTY

17

BEING AWAY AT COLLEGE changed Jill's perspective of her last few years at home. At first, only a chance remark in her letters showed this change. Then with increasing frequency, she wrote more, asking "Why did I do that? What was wrong with me?"

Now it was her turn to say "I don't understand," as though she only had some vague recollection of the girl who had hidden inside that protective cocoon. She was trying to get a clear picture of what had happened to that girl and how she felt, but she could no longer get her into focus.

When I refused to carry the responsibility for Jill's actions any longer, it was for myself, not her. I had to be free of the overwhelming guilt. But once Gene and I let go, Jill was forced to come to terms with herself. She discovered no one had ever made her be good or bad. She had always chosen her own behavior.

I suppose the conclusion was inevitable. If she made her own decisions, if she alone was responsible, then she was also guilty. I ached for her as I saw this happen. I knew what it was to struggle under a backpack of guilt. I did not want that for her.

Once before, Jill had tried to accept responsibility for her actions. During our required counseling, she had told her caseworker, "It's not my parents. It's me!" But, as Jill told us later, "She didn't listen to me. All she ever asked was, 'Did you have any fights this week? What did they say? What did you say?'" So the moment passed.

Now the realization had returned. Only this time she was away from home, separated from everything familiar. I wanted to help her as I sensed the pain in her letters.

Maybe I could share the gift of freedom I had found. Yet I was uncertain just how close I could move toward her. Then Gene and I received this letter, and I knew the hole in our wall was big enough to reach through.

Dear Mom and Dad,

You couldn't know all the times I wish I was at home in my own room with my parents just across the hall. And I think of the nights I lay awake craving to go in and talk, but something—pride, maybe—always held me back. Now I think how I wasted three years that could've been filled with love. . . .

I guess it takes a long time to realize how much someone means to you—too long to learn appreciation and gratitude. And it probably seems like an infinity to those who are waiting to have their love accepted and reciprocated. . . .

I have a terrible fear that something will happen to you before I can make up for the past, before you know I love you. I lie awake at night crying because it shouldn't be this way.

146

I am still just a child, but I am growing. Someday I hope to have as full and meaningful a life as you have shown me. Most of all, I hope to find someone to love and be loved by as much as you do each other. With that kind of power, what else matters?

Someday you will know . . .

I love you.

Jill

And so, I began to convey my acceptance and forgiveness in terms we both understood. I reminded her of her favorite movie, *Love Story,* and related the theme to ourselves: Love means you never have to say you're sorry. I returned to the prodigal son: The boy just knew he could go home. He knew his father loved him, and he didn't carry his guilt any farther than his father's arms. He dumped it by the side of the road and went into the party.

We worried about Jill. Was counseling available at school if she needed it? Would Eddie be tempted to get her started on drugs now that even he must realize she was changing? The wide-open concept of dormitory life afforded her little protection.

But, unknown to us, Jill was trying to make a break with Eddie. Now that she was thinking differently, she was afraid of him. When she moved from her old dormitory, she avoided telling him, and she asked her roommate to stay in the room if he ever showed up.

One day, Eddie did come. Karen left the room for a minute, and he took out a knife. He never threatened Jill; never even alluded to the knife, just handled it. After he had gone, Jill lay on her bed shaking. She still didn't know what she wanted, but she was becoming more clear on what she didn't want to be involved in.

That summer between her freshman and sophomore years at Indiana U, we began to talk again. Jill had gotten a job in the coffee shop at Welborn Baptist Hospital. Sometimes after working all day, she would put in some hours at the Village Inn. I sympathized with her exhaustion and stopped hassling over her messes. After seeing her room empty for so long, the clutter was almost welcome. Jill no longer seemed to search out irritating behaviors.

It was a good summer for both of us. The only controversy was whether Jill could live off campus in the fall. We felt more secure with her in a dorm, particularly since she had moved last semester to one with slightly more control. She had made that decision herself, wanting to find a place more conducive to study.

But now we could talk about it. We could state our opinions, give our reasons, and still listen to Jill. And she could accept what we said without resentment. When we said we could only afford the dormitory costs, she recognized this as a financial fact rather than a form of coercion. She was willing to economize to live in an apartment. So we helped her assemble the things she needed to keep house: dishcloths, towels, a toaster, and a twin bed. Then we rented a trailer and moved her back to Bloomington.

The girl Jill was to share an apartment with had lived there all summer. It was obvious she didn't like housekeeping. I realized the apartment even looked bad to Jill, as she made excuses for its appearance and explained how she could fix it up. Then Jill discovered her bedroom would be the dining room, a tiny room between the living room and the only bedroom and kitchen. The bathroom opened off the dining room, too. Jill would have little privacy. There weren't even doors to close her room off.

Together we unloaded the trailer. I didn't want to leave her there. And so it became one more time of letting go. If I said anything, Jill would feel defensive. Our whole summer would be wasted. So I said nothing.

Outside that dingy little apartment, I put my arms around my daughter. I felt she had to be disappointed and embarrassed. For the first time in several years, I held her close. And she hugged back.

In the car, I moaned, "Oh, honey!"

"I know!" Gene replied.

Jill was trying so hard to be her own person and make her own decisions. Why did they have to turn out like this?

Later, Jill's new roommate let her older brother move into the living room. Jill called and told us she was moving back into the dorm at semester break. Would we come and haul her things back home?

When we picked her up that day, she was happy and excited. She wanted us to stop and get a term paper she had written about our family traditions. She was anxious to share it with us, because we had all contributed to it. Earlier that semester, she had come home and interviewed each of us with a tape recorder. She had even sent tapes to Grandma Ton and Grandma Williams with questions for them to answer.

In the guise of doing a paper on folklore, Jill had opened herself to our love. We were woven together again as we talked about lighting candles on the Advent wreath, baking cookies and stollen, reading our favorite stories, and singing carols.

As Jill wrote that paper, she rediscovered many old memories. She became aware of her loneliness in the last few years. No wonder she climbed into the car so eagerly: she was in a hurry to get home!

It didn't hurt that the paper rated an *A* and a handwritten message from the instructor, "Very well done!" Of course it was well done. It was Jill's claim to her inheritance—the same inheritance we had banked on when we said, "Run away, little girl." Now Jill was running at breakneck speed toward home. The five of us were saying in every way we knew how, *It's been such a long time. We've missed you. Come on in to the party.*

EPILOGUE

SOME STORIES END WITH "And they lived happily ever after." I can't honestly write those words.

My children continue to choose their own life-styles, sometimes diametrically opposed to mine. But letting go comes easier now, and the dividends are worth the effort. Because I have given each of them the freedom to say no, I have heard them say their own yes. Once they feel safe with me, they have opened themselves, and I have come to know them as persons.

Through the writing of this book, Jill and I have looked inside each other. I have discovered things I never knew before, and she knows more about me. I have experienced a real tenderness for the girl who used to be—the girl who turned my neat little life upside down. We have gone through this story bit by bit with Jill sitting cross-legged on the bed, sharing her own reflections. As I've listened, I've been amazed at how little I have known of my daughter.

I have so much to thank her for. Because of Jill, I have grown. Do you remember the old custom of birthday spankings—one, two, three, and one to grow on? I count my children in much the same way. One is for Jack, two for Jeff, three is for Joe—three boys—and one to grow on—Jill. I have jokingly told friends I ought to have another baby, because now I have learned how to be a parent.

The writing of this story is Jill's and my attempt to throw a lifeline to other parents and their children. It has not been easy to write. There is a lot of ugliness. I have often wondered what my friends will think when they read what I have written. Will they still like me or Jill? Will their illusions about a pastor's family be destroyed? At those times, I've wondered if there wasn't some way to call the whole thing off. But last Maundy Thursday two friends of mine sat next to me in church. The wife leaned over and whispered, "Our Christie is gone again, and we don't know where she is." In their faces, I saw the anguish I had known. And I knew why our story had to be told.

I wanted to tell them all I had learned these past few years. I wanted to say, don't let her do to you what I see happening. Don't allow her to become your center. It will close in on you, until your life is crushed. That's a terrible responsibility for her to bear. Let your life center around each other, your home, your *now,* and your future. Discover some way to grow as a person. There is so little of yourself left right now; no wonder you don't have anything to give her. Grow toward the you God intended—in freedom and trust.

Share with her the beauty of your past together, not only the ugliness of now. She remembers those precious memories and is still the same person. Affirm this side of her, believe in it, act on it. She needs to know that you see the scared little girl behind her mask.

Open yourselves to healing by exposing your hurt to others. Don't be ashamed; people care that you are hurting. Let them minister to you with the gifts the Holy Spirit has given them. A wound covered up festers deeper and deeper. Opening it allows the poison to drain. Certainly some won't understand. They will think something's got to be the matter with you, or your child wouldn't turn out like that. Never mind about them. There are those who will say, "Oh, yes, I know exactly what you're feeling. I've been there too."

Just the other day I sat at my kitchen table and shared a part of this story with my mother. I told her how I had come to feel about myself and how I had thought of suicide. She cried and said, "But I never knew. . . . I never even knew." Never again will I refuse to let God love me through the ministry of the Christian community. Never again will I hesitate to be that community for someone else.

I am so proud of the young woman who is my daughter. Never have I seen new birth—new life—evidenced more clearly. She doesn't equate her change in those theological terms. But I do. You see, we're still two different people.